W9-ARA-612

HAPPINESS ROAD

ALICE HEGAN RICE

HAPPINESS ROAD

Essay Index Reprint Series

BOOKS FOR LIBRARIES PRESS
FREEPORT, NEW YORK

Reprinted 1968 by arrangement with
Appleton-Century, affiliate of Meredith Press

LIBRARY OF CONGRESS CATALOG CARD NUMBER:
68-58810

PRINTED IN THE UNITED STATES OF AMERICA

A Foreword

A FEW weeks before Alice Hegan Rice died she said, "If anything should happen to me will you finish my book?" We were walking up and down our living room at the time, a habit we enjoyed between spells of reading aloud, and her words were as near as we ever approached the inevitable realization that one of us must go first.

Into this book, a brave and beautiful attempt to help others, she had been putting her heart, and each day I had begrudged the effort she was making. But she loved the mere act of writing so much, and had been so limited in her other activities by a long cardiac trouble, that, whatever my anxiety, I always intervened with great reluctance. Too, she counted herself a happy, fortunate woman, and it is more than a consolation to know that she could continue writing happily almost to the end.

Through many years she had gathered into her notebooks the wise and spiritual sayings of those who had practised and written about the art of right living, thinking and helping. It is many of these sayings that she has incorporated, together with her own thoughts, into these brief essays. *My Pillow Book,* a predecessor to this volume, had given so many comfort that I think she looked forward keenly to giving further help. But the writing here is with a difference, for it embodies also the influence of her psychological reading.

I had gone over with her the greater part of *Happiness Road* before the end came, so its completion involved little difficulty. Sometimes her notes were confused, but she knew I would understand them and that though our philosophies differed in many respects, I should be able to say what was intended.

She lived largely by faith; I by whatever insight, knowledge and reason were at my command. Nor do I think either of us would have had it otherwise. That she was the rarest being I have ever known, I have never doubted. That she has enriched the lives of so many comforted her, and that this book, too, might do so was her dear hope.

CALE YOUNG RICE

Louisville, Kentucky

Acknowledgments

For their kindness in allowing the use of certain quotations in this book, the publisher wishes to thank the following:

Alfred A. Knopf, Inc., for permission to quote on pages 39, 43, 50, and 58 lines from *The Prophet*, by Kahlil Gibran;

Little, Brown and Company, for permission to quote a stanza by Emily Dickinson on page 45;

The Macmillan Company, for permission to quote on page 23 an excerpt from *New Pathways in Science*, by Sir Arthur Eddington; and

Estate of S. Weir Mitchell, for permission to quote lines by Dr. Mitchell on page 101.

Contents

HAPPINESS ROAD

Happiness Road

FROM the dawn of civilization humanity has been following a trail whose end is ever lost in the heights. Stumbling, falling, and fighting, men have struggled valiantly on in the quest of happiness.

Each generation and each race has sought it after its own fashion and each has found it for brief seasons only to lose it again. Egypt built great tombs for her dead to enjoy through eternity. Greece tried to discover happiness in the pursuit of beauty and truth. India sought to capture it by the suppression of all desire.

Some philosophers have taught that moderation is the secret of happiness; others that giving rein to the pleasures of the senses is the means of achieving it. Still others have declared that it is only through the pleasures of the mind that happiness is to be found.

The early Christians held that happiness lay in minimizing the conditions of this life and in living for the glories of the world to come. Not until the Renaissance was this hope of the future combined with a full appreciation of the beauty and worthwhileness of human life.

With the discovery of the New World men sought happiness in physical activity—in wresting comfort and safety out of the wilderness. But the Puritans made the mistake of disassociating happiness and religion, of looking upon gaiety as shallowness and upon merriment as frivolity, wholly missing the truth known to the prophets of old that "the joy of the Lord is our strength."

What then is the true nature of this happiness men have lived and died for? We know one thing for certain. Happiness is not a mere temporary, selfish pleasure that excites and exhilarates for a moment, but it lies in a state of mind. Also we know that there is a technic in attaining it. Yet while we devote years to the study of the arts, we give little attention to the most important of all the arts, that of achieving a happy life.

There are brilliant men and women the world over who have attained greatness in their respective fields yet who in their secret souls are dissatisfied, thwarted, and disillusioned. They have been so busy achieving personal ambitions that they have overlooked the supremely enjoyable obligation of finding happiness. On the other hand there are radiant personalities who go singing their way through life, sometimes under the most trying circumstances, yet whose very happiness helps and blesses all with whom they come in contact. They have learned that happiness is a by-product of right living and thinking, a result of our spiritual adjustment to circumstances. That it must never be regarded as the chief aim in life but only as a just and fundamental need of mankind.

In ordinary circumstances we start out in life being happy. Children are gay under a blazing tropic sun or in the freezing blasts of the arctic. They build toy houses on the edge of a volcano or play tag on a battlefield. But with maturity comes knowledge and with knowledge fear.

It is then that we must trust no longer to Nature, but consciously take control of our lives and live according to a fixed purpose. At first we invariably follow false trails, asking merely material approaches to our goal. We want money, fame, success; and if we get them we frequently find ourselves landed in bogs of idleness, selfishness, and unfulfilled ambition. But gradually along the rocky gorges of sorrow, down the stony paths of temptation, and in the valleys of disillusionment, we realize that happiness and peace are only to be found upon a different road.

While each individual must of necessity approach his problem from his own personal angle, there are a few broad principles that may be followed.

First, it is necessary for us to keep in mind that any pursuit of happiness contrary to the common good is doomed to failure. Second, that even though disease and sorrow are all about us, health and happiness are the normal state of man. Third, that happiness is a duty, not only because of its effect upon us but because of its influence upon others.

To each thinking adult come hours of discouragement, depression, and despair. Were it not so we would never seek to right the wrongs that exist all about us. But it is possible so to build our characters, develop our abilities, and discipline our moods, that we can attain an integrated personality which no change of fortune can permanently affect.

One may well ask how we dare speak of happiness in this war-torn world, so full of cruelty, suffering, hatred, and death.

The answer is clear. America is probably the one nation in the world to-day where the great traditions of life and of beautiful living may still be maintained. It is our privilege and duty to keep those high ideals alive, to cultivate and hoard the joy and peace and serenity of life, in order to pass them on to a saddened and embittered humanity. Unless as individuals and as a nation we strive unceasingly to establish and preserve a sane, progressive, humanitarian civilization, chaos is inevitable.

The way to attain this ideal is not easy. Each day is a challenge to our faith, courage, and steadfast purpose. We must approach the problem with mature intelligence and yet with the open-mindedness of children, giving up preconceived notions and arrogant dogmas, and substituting a humility that is willing to learn.

In the attempt to transmit suggestion which may be useful to fellow travelers along the Happiness Road, I am here but a medium. Sometimes the messages are my own, often they come from minds far wiser than mine. Little that is new can be said concerning the eternal verities. Therefore, as has often been said, the only thing that can justify a writer in adding to the multitude of books already written on the subject is that life has never before been seen through his particular eyes.

For that reason there is always a chance, if we be wholly sincere, that some gleam, however feeble, may be transmitted through us along the way to some one struggling through the darkness toward the light.

Stock Taking

SOCRATES' dictum "Know thyself" is as sound to-day as when it was uttered. Before any undertaking is attempted, it is wise to decide exactly what we seek, and how well we are equipped to achieve it.

Evelyn Underhill, the English mystic, says: "Religion demands a drastic overhauling of the elements of character, a real repentance, and moral purgation, as the beginning of all spiritual truth."

So let us put away all personal pride, arrogance and egotism and try humbly to see ourselves as we really are. For we must consider whether we are trained by discipline and habit to meet the hardships of our journey through life, where there will be steep hills to climb and grave obstacles to overcome. Our hands must be quick to minister to the needs of others, our feet swift to run errands of mercy, our shoulders strong to bear not only our own burdens but those of our weaker brothers.

In order to meet life successfully we must study our own physical needs, and then coöperate to the fullest with science to correct unfavorable conditions for others. Having got our bodies in the best possible running order, we can then examine our minds.

Here we encounter more subtle and difficult conditions. Modern psychology has done much to help us in self-analysis and the correction of maladjustments. Many theories have been advanced, from Freud's conviction that all neuroses are sexual in origin, to Bergson's belief that they are largely a matter of infantile fixation. We are told that egotism and ignorance are the contributing causes to most mental sickness; that emotional instability, the very quality necessary to artists, poets and musicians, can, if not controlled, prove one of the most destructive factors in life.

In taking stock of our mental attributes, each of us must ask himself the following questions:

Do I suffer from a sense of inferiority? If so, perhaps that is because I can not have the dominance I desire over others.

Do I feel superior to others? Then I must be arrogant and conceited and insistent upon people accepting me at my own valuation.

Am I hypersensitive? Then I am probably thinking more of myself than others, and demanding more consideration.

Have I stopped growing? To be fixed in habit, thought, or environment is to share the fate of a fossil.

What do I fear? Most of us suffer from some form of phobia, which weakens our initiative, decreases our ability, and limits our usefulness. Do I?

These are searching questions, but it is only when they are honestly faced that we can even begin to know ourselves.

Many people find the world cold, indifferent, and unkind, not realizing that the cause lies directly in themselves. An inward glance will often reveal our own lack of tenderness, compassion, and thoughtfulness.

Another source of unhappiness is the habit of imputing ignoble motives to others, motives of which we consider ourselves incapable. We give a tactless word, an indifferent glance, a graceless act, a significance that was never intended.

Far more important than the body or the mind, in making an inventory of ourselves, is giving an account of our spiritual state. The true test of spiritual efficiency is whether or not we live up to our full capacity, whether we are idly drifting with the current, or are using every physical, mental, and spiritual quality we possess to the utmost of our ability.

Whatever thing we want most in life is, in truth, our religion, be it fame, wealth, health, or goodness. It is a law of our nature that when an end has been effectively suggested to the unconscious mind, that mind tends to work toward its realization.

At the very start of our spiritual journey it is of paramount importance therefore to define our goal, and then discard all hampering impedimenta that may prevent our reaching it.

Burdens

CONSIDERING the useless burdens we carry through life, it is a wonder we ever survive. Old sorrows, remorses, dead hopes, unfulfilled desires, hatreds, rebellions, all weigh down our hearts and deaden our minds.

One of the worst of these burdens is worry; not the legitimate anxiety that senses danger ahead and sets about intelligently to avoid it, but the useless worry over things that can not be helped.

Our burdens are of many kinds, those that are inflicted upon us, and those we assume. Our own all too frequently come from self-centeredness, the failure to realize that we do not exist solely to be well and successful, but chiefly to carry out the divine plan under whatever circumstances we find ourselves.

The woman who said, "I haven't the courage to be unhappy," expressed a true, if satirical, fact. The tendency to make idols of our loved ones, to expect perfection in ourselves or others, to brood over the things that happen, lead inevitably to wretchedness.

It is necessary to realize that everything is relative, contingent on circumstances, temperament, the human element. We have only to place our personal vexations beside the momentous issues of life to find that they frequently dwindle to trifles.

Whatever the nature of our burdens, we must guard

against trying to carry more than we are capable of. The weight is largely regulated by our personal reaction; the stolid unimaginative man can bear a load that would break the spirit of a highly sensitive, sympathetic one. But even the latter can learn to face issues with calmness, to derive satisfaction from discharging moral obligations, and to accept self-sacrifice cheerfully.

The problem of carrying another's burdens is a difficult one. While compassion compels us to ease another's load wherever we can, it is necessary for us to remember that by taking on some one else's responsibility and assuming his obligations, we are depriving him of his only chance of development. It is just as bad to be unduly leaned upon as it is to lean. Self-sacrifice often results in making parasites of others. "Losing one's life" does not mean making ourselves futile and unhappy by useless self-surrender. Often we can not really bear another's burden; we can only break our hearts in the attempt. The so-called duty that keeps us in bondage—unfits us for the performance of our own job in life—can make us in turn a burden to others and deprive us of the joy of living. It should never be regarded as obligatory.

There are, however, legitimate burdens which no self-respecting person may shirk. They may be grievously heavy and desperately hard to bear, but whether they are laid upon us or self-assumed, they can only be successfully handled by sublimation. Perhaps the very tragedy you are called upon to face is one that no other person can handle. You may be the one medium in the whole world through whom God can perform a delicate task. By meeting the situation in an ideal way and preserving your own faith and integrity in doing so, you establish an ideal for all others who face a similar problem.

Does not this give even a grievous burden a dignity—a glory—that makes it a privilege to bear?

Humility

I come in the little things
Saith the Lord:
My starry wings
I do forsake,
Love's highway of humility to take.

EVELYN UNDERHILL

RUSKIN declared that the first test of a truly great man is his humility. But by humility he did not mean a supine acceptance of good and evil alike. Though the most humble of all men was capable of anger and strong language, given to passionate repudiation of wrong, indignant at injustice, intolerant of hypocrisy, rebellious against inequalities, He could nevertheless say to those who would worship Him, "Why callest me good? There is none good but one, that is God."

Before the time of Christ the word humility was a term of contempt. To be humble meant being weak or cowardly, just as meekness still carries a cringing connotation. It suggested having a poor opinion of one's self, an attitude considered absurd until Christ came to prove otherwise.

Throughout the Gospels the new meaning of the word was accepted, and humility came to be regarded as "the sweet root from which all heavenly virtues shoot." It presupposed a life of inner simplicity, that reckoned worth, not by material standards, but by its intrinsic value.

Intellectuality combined with arrogance is one of the deadliest hindrances to humility. There are many mental giants who are spiritual pigmies. Nothing can so obstruct a man's vision as his own ego. It prompts him to set a false value on personal achievement, and demand that the world's valuation coincide with his own.

Tagore stresses throughout his teachings the necessity of knowing the soul apart from the self. He goes so far as to say that sin is the defeat of a man's soul by his self. Now this self, which we think we know so well, is really a mysterious thing, beguiling us with its importance, deluding us into the belief that it is the ultimate goal of our desires. Sometimes it appeals to us on the physical side, concerning itself with the importance of physical health. Again, it is a mental preoccupation, bent on acquiring knowledge for utterly selfish reasons. Sometimes it is absorbed in saving its own soul to the exclusion of all others.

Thomas à Kempis gives us the key to self-knowledge when he says: "He who truly knows himself, is lowly in his own eyes." We have but to compare ourselves as we are with what we might be, to be humbled. "By matching ourselves against ourselves are we shamed."

But however humble we may be we should never forget that a cipher placed beside a unit materially changes its value. By alining ourselves with the Infinite we can enhance our value tenfold.

Will Durant says: "Ask too much and it shall be

denied you, knock too loudly and it shall not be opened unto you, seek impatiently and you shall not find."

One who has spiritually discerned the truth has little need for the dogma of theologians. The humblest, simplest soul may know more of God than all the sages can teach.

If you honestly believe that nothing in you is too good to devote to the lowest, then you have found the humble way to the highest. The capacity of the soul to be used is all that really counts.

Education means acknowledging a higher intellect, submitting to mental discipline in order to achieve knowledge. But Cowper points out, "Knowledge is proud that it has learned, but wisdom is humble that it knows no more."

"If I could choose a young man's companions," wrote Phillips Brooks, "some should be weaker than himself, that he might learn patience and charity; many should be as nearly as possible his equals, that he might have the full freedom of friendship; but most should be stronger than he, that he might forever be thinking humbly of himself and be tempted to higher things."

Duty

UNFORTUNATELY, the word duty has acquired a disagreeable connotation. This is probably due to the fact that we prefer goodness to be based on choice rather than on obligation. As responsibilities to self, family, city, state, and country come to each of us, it is a never-ending problem as to which are imperative and which we are best fitted to fulfil.

We have been told that duties never conflict; but few of us can subscribe to the truth of this. To be sure, the physician's first care is the preservation of the body; the preacher's, saving the soul; but neither can be exclusive. Our Savior had a supreme duty on earth, but he was ever ready to respond to the faintest call of need. Love is universal and can not be limited to one person, one thing, one cause.

Often, in other days, the tendency was to stress altruism at the expense of individualism. The family took precedence over everything else. Many men and women who would have been of inestimable value to the world were sacrificed on the altar of family duty. Incompatible people were expected to live under one roof, invading each other's privacy, irritating each other in countless small ways, when by living separately they might possibly have found pleasure in a less intimate companionship. Domination of parents, rebellious submission of children, the presence of uncongenial relatives were all part of the old mistaken idea of doing one's so-called duty at any cost.

Many acts of apparent unselfishness, when viewed in the light of their ultimate outcome, bring sorrow to those for whom the sacrifice was made. We can not live another's life for him any more than he can live ours for us. We can only wreck ourselves in the effort. "It is no use being a saint to-day," some one has said, "if you are going to be a burden to-morrow."

There are certain unfortunate people who prey upon others, vitiating their strength, demanding their pity, using them as receptacles for their stored-up bitterness, but refusing their counsel or constructive suggestions.

So long as we can help such people to a higher level we should keep on trying, but when we find that instead of our lifting them, they are pulling us down, we may be sure that we are either performing our task in the wrong spirit or that our duty lies elsewhere.

The swing from altruism to individualism has been marked in recent years, and the tendency to shirk responsibility is as bad as the acceptance of useless obligations.

Too many people are relegating the care of their children to others, shifting the aged and infirm from the home to an institution, sidestepping any obligation that interferes with personal freedom.

One should lead one's own life only in so far as it is compatible with the welfare of others, but this can not be accomplished on the dry basis of duty alone. We must bring something far more tender and understanding to the task.

There are certain sacred obligations which none of us can afford to neglect. The duty health owes to illness, strength to weakness, joy to misery. How better can we acknowledge a blessing than by being mindful of the one who has it not?

Courage

Courage leads starward, fear toward death.

SENECA

A stout heart breaks bad luck.

CERVANTES

Life is mostly froth and bubble,
Two things stand like stone—
Kindness in another's trouble,
Courage in your own.

A. L. GORDON

"COURAGE," says Fosdick, "is adventuring life for a possibility, faith is believing the possibility really exists." It is a tribute to humanity when we say that courage is one of its commonest attributes, for in its soil most of the other virtues have their roots.

Whatever the burden we are called upon to bear, it is the way we take it that determines its weight. Existence is beset with difficulties; from the beginning men have been pitted against difficult circumstances, forced to struggle in order to survive, to suffer in order to grow. Out of these hardships sprang our fears—of sickness, poverty, failure—and our progress depended upon whether we cowered helpless before these destructive thoughts or courageously grappled with them.

Fear is one of the most important of primitive instincts. First given to animals for self-protection, it poured adrenalin into their blood to enable them to fight or flee. But man's reaction to fear, when not resulting in fight or flight, degenerates into worry, anxiety, and depression, on which adrenalin has no effect.

Rightly considered, fear is a warning upon which we should act intelligently, neither disregarding it nor allowing it to dominate us. Radicals may be as lacking in courage when they fear to conform as conservatives in fearing to deviate from the accepted path. The unthinking optimist is as bad as the unthinking pessimist. In both cases a surface view is taken, not informed by truth but by the mood or temperament of the individual. We can be hopeful without being complacent; discouraged without being hopeless.

When we fail to meet the challenge life presents to us, our first inclination is to seek an alibi. We claim that under different circumstances we could have been finer and wiser. The truth is that if affliction has taught us nothing, if strength has not come out of the struggle and wisdom out of experience, the fault is ours.

To be sure, if we never climb we will never fall, if we never strive we will never be disappointed. But the static life of a parasite is one accepted only by the morally defective.

It is only by facing whatever comes, not as something to be met with supine resignation, but as a challenge to our intelligence and resourcefulness, that we can release the energy and ability latent within us.

The depressed state of mind of a chronic pessimist is the inevitable sign of cowardice. His negative attitude, his lack of faith, his absorption in self, foredoom him to failure. His worries and anxieties affect not only himself but all with whom he comes in contact.

Courage is never associated with a passive acquiescence. It is ever striving toward something higher, willing to accept a painful experience if it can lead to a finer issue.

One of the first steps toward a positive, confident life is the recognition that Nature is an ally rather than a foe. "The body tends to health, the Spirit tends to peace." Everything aims at survival, and toward this end there is ever a wise adaptation of life to new conditions.

It is well to keep in mind that the life principle is equipped to meet the most difficult emergencies. It has enabled man to struggle up from the mire through inexpressible hardships, constantly to develop new resources, and find adequate methods of adjustment. It tends to surmount every difficulty, persevere against every discouragement.

While this life principle of preservation and adaptability has been going on since long before the advent of man, it is only in comparatively recent times that we have learned to work with it and hasten the process of evolution. When physicians discovered that men can be physically brave yet at the same time spiritually craven; that our spiritual muscles are as dependent on exercise as physical ones; they began to treat the body as a mental and spiritual as well as a physical entity.

Hospitals all over the land are crowded with neurotic patients who are being reëducated to a new way of thinking and living. It is no longer necessary to clench our fists, grit our teeth and stiffen our backs for the next blow. That is the physical part of courage. But we are learning that a better way is consciously to cooperate with the indwelling Spirit, thereby releasing those dynamic qualities of courage, faith, and love that make for healthy, successful living.

Faith

Bid then the tender light of faith to shine
By which alone the mortal heart is led
Unto the thinking of the thought divine.

GEORGE SANTAYANA

OF all the qualities of the human mind by far the most creative is faith. It is by faith alone that religion and science come into being. A man must believe in something even if it is only in his ability to disbelieve. In these days of skepticism the word faith is too often linked with the adjective "blind." Those who tend to believe only what they can perceive with the senses or explain on a purely intellectual basis are apt to look upon faith as something based on ignorance and superstition.

What these people fail to perceive is that all science was once faith, and that all great achievements had their motivation in the belief that a thing could be accomplished before it was attempted.

The modern miracles which science has performed, such as the discovery and use of electricity, have yielded such practical results that we are apt to lose sight of their spiritual significance. Belief in principle and Providence has been crowded out by our concern with the visible details of materiality.

The absurdity of saying we will believe nothing that

we can not prove is self-evident. Authorities differ as to what constitutes truth, some going so far as to say there is no such thing as absolute truth. If the latter are right, the Christian's belief in the efficacy of faith is quite as tenable as the skeptic's conjectures.

The two approaches to faith, by reason and intuition, are both necessary, but in matters pertaining to the spirit, the soul must ever take precedence over the intellect. Intuition rather than reason opens the channel through which the individual touches the universal.

It is interesting to note the belief among modern thinkers in something that has never been proved. Whitehead and Eddington in physics, Myers in biology, Haldane in philosophy, Jeans in astronomy, McDougal and William James in psychology, all men preeminent in their various professions, are convinced of a rational and predetermining influence in the universe.

To quote from but a few, Sir Arthur Eddington declares:

". . . When from the human heart . . . the cry goes up, 'What is it all about?' it is no true answer to look only at that part of experience which comes to us through certain sensory organs and reply: 'It is about atoms and chaos; it is about a universe of fiery globes rolling on to impending doom; it is about . . . non-commutative algebra.' Rather, it is about a spirit in which truth has its shrine, with potentialities of self-fulfilment in its response to beauty and right."

Sir James Jeans says:

"We discover that the universe shows evidence of a

designing or controlling power that has something in common with our own individual minds."

Henri Bergson goes even further in stating that "we are partners with God in our creative evolution."

If we accept, with such great thinkers, the fact of an intelligence back of the universe, then we must believe in a moral order in the world, and consequently, in the final triumph of good.

No teaching that is not based on reason can be tolerated by critical minds, but the belief that an accident of blind force produces this highly organized world is far more fantastic than the theory that a Super Intelligence devised its ordered evolution.

The infallible test of a man's religion or philosophy is, "Does it work?" In science there are endless hypotheses; in metaphysics as many theories as there are exponents. But unless these things in some way contribute to the betterment of humanity, or affect our conduct, they can have little ultimate value.

"Faith," says Dean Inge, "begins as an experiment, but ends as an experience." Whenever we yield to its urge, new and exciting adventures open to us. A blind Milton, a deaf Beethoven, believing in their genius, rose above circumstance and made their belief a reality.

The law of teleology teaches that the desire is drawn toward fulfilment the moment the end is clearly perceived. Faith, unfortunately, seldom shines continuously. The guiding light beckons us on, then flickers out. There are periods of darkness in every life that threaten spiritual annihilation.

To-day the world has disappointed and betrayed us. The things we have lived for, sacrificed for, and passionately believed in are being ruthlessly trampled underfoot. Even the teachings of Christ are swept aside as impractical, visionary, sentimental.

Yet despite the materialism, pessimism, and disillusionment all about us, we know that the nobility of life remains intact. Heroic sacrifice, incomparable courage, faith in the ultimate triumph of good were never more manifest than in the present struggle.

The supreme test of faith comes in our belief in a life hereafter. Which conjecture seems the more intelligent—that we should go into oblivion taking with us all that life has taught us in this life, or that we should go on growing and giving in another life, retaining the love we have given and received in this?

Again we can fall back on the fact that the heart's desire works toward its own fulfilment. Since survival has been the supreme desire of man since his creation, perhaps Lowell is right when he says that "the longing to be so, helps make the soul immortal."

Creative Thinking

DARE to launch out on life's uncharted sea, for in you the Great Pilot, the Great Adventurer, the Great Poet, the Great Inventor, the Great Musician, the Great Artist, is making Its quest for individual experience. Genius springs from the soul that dares to drink at the fountains of inspiration in the garden of God.

FENWICK HOLMES

THE two minds of man, the conscious and the subconscious, function in different ways. The latter is the builder of the body, ceaselessly directing its activities, and compelling it to reproduce its kind. This mind is impersonal, deductive, with no purpose of its own, but being clairvoyant and clairaudient, it serves as a medium through which we contact the universal.

It is the conscious mind that fashions the thought which the unconscious mind brings into existence in form. The cells of our body, which are constantly made and replaced by the unconscious mind, are under the influence of the conscious mind, and reflect its attitude toward good and evil, health and disease.

The power to choose our thoughts and direct them, therefore, constitutes a partial free will, which enables us by the power of suggestion to modify many of our inherited or environmental tendencies.

This freedom, however, has its disadvantages, for

we are free to choose unwisely as well as wisely. Our bodies act on very old instincts and the animal in us clamors for satisfaction.

Whether our instincts are prompted by sex, self-preservation, or frustration, it is the use we make of them that determines our character. Following the primal impulses leads to degeneracy; denying them results in illness; directing them in channels consonant with spiritual living results in health and peace.

The discovery that it is in our power to change our lives by the thoughts we think is the first step toward spiritual mastery. Life takes on a grave responsibility when we realize that our minds, like our bodies, grow by what they feed upon, and that it devolves upon us to furnish the proper nourishment. Bergson says, "In a conscious being to exist is to change, to change is to mature, to mature is to go on creating ourselves endlessly."

Whatever we give our attention to is the thing that governs us. If our mental searchlight seeks out the mean, the sordid, the ugly, we reflect those qualities in our lives. The only excuse for preoccupation with such things is a desire to change conditions.

Each of us is supreme ruler over one kingdom and that is his own mind. We make our decisions, change them, select our thoughts, and are responsible for our emotional reaction to the outer world.

The fallacy of believing that right thinking will banish disease, poverty and unhappiness is manifest. But by conscious effort we can minimize these disasters and emerge from them triumphant.

The law of correspondence is that the universe assumes to us just the attitude we take toward it. When we utter a pessimistic thought or an unjust criticism, we create an atmosphere that immediately affects us as well as others.

The greatest of American psychologists claims that if we make the right appeal to any human faculty, that faculty will expand and begin to grow. To what extent do we call forth the best in our fellow men?

The majority of people live without a plan. They go through life accepting other people's creeds, other people's moral and social ideals, following ever the line of least resistance. The mind, a powerful machine, built for a useful purpose, is too often allowed to whirl in undirected futility.

There is no better way of directing our thoughts than by intelligent use of imagination. By clearly visualizing our ideals and holding them before us to the exclusion of all baser and more ignoble desires, we best attain our end. Virtue, like sin, is first conceived in the mind, and psychologists tell us that imagination is a more powerful factor than will-power in character building.

Whatever discouragement we may feel as to our ability to be of use in the world should be minimized when we realize that no one has ever had our exact inheritance and environment, and that we may be fitted to perform a task no one else can accomplish. Such a thought fires the imagination and makes us eager to discover just what our peculiar mission in the world may be. It is well to remember that each of us is a link in a chain that reaches back through centuries, and that upon our weakness or strength depends the nature of the links to come.

The preoccupation of helping to make a better world lifts us above petty, personal vanities, jealousies, and self-preoccupations, and enables us to bring into being the finer things we desire.

The instinct to create springs directly out of the unconscious mind, and the finer the model presented, the finer the thing produced.

Thomas Edison says: "As I analyze my reactions to thoughts and ideas which appear in my mind, I feel that the mere fact that I have an idea is proof that the same source that gave me the idea will also show me how to work it out, provided I hold on."

Napoleon Bonaparte claimed to have fought every battle in his imagination on the eve of the actual engagement. Disraeli held the vision of himself as Prime Minister of England until, against heavy odds, he achieved his ambition.

Practical demonstration of the power of suggestion can be made in everyday life. By fighting through our crises in advance, rehearsing our parts in accordance with our highest ideals, we can perform them, when the time comes, with poise and wisdom.

Suggestion affects others quite as much as it affects us. There is no limit to what we may accomplish with the aid of imagination. As the sculptor apprehends an angel in a block of stone; the musician a symphony in a bird song; the poet God in a wild flower, so we can discern hidden beauties in our fellow men, and help to draw them forth.

Jesus Christ, more than any one else who ever lived, exercised this creative power, calling forth the potential goodness in the most depraved of his fellow men, and by claiming them as brothers established their right to be the sons of God.

Joy

THESE things have I spoken unto you, that my joy might remain in you, and that your joy might be full.

JOHN XV:11

WHAT a magnificent bequest to mankind! And what superb courage coming from one cruelly persecuted and facing a death of ignominy! Nothing could more fully reveal the victorious power of divine joy to triumph over pain and despair and dominate the darkest situation.

Let us consider some of the aspects of joy. It is not something we can achieve by pursuing; it is rather something born in the heart out of a divine companionship and overflowing in a life in harmony with the life of God. Independent of outer circumstance, regardless of wealth or poverty, health or sickness, it visits the soul prepared to welcome it.

The well balanced life has been defined as one-third work, one-third religion and one-third play. Unfortunately the importance of the last is sometimes minimized by the overzealous Christian who is apt to associate gaiety and merriment with frivolity. The Puritan belief that goodness must walk with a dull and solemn tread has been one of the most disastrous factors in the religion of America. Knocking on wood when we make an optimistic statement is a sorry survival of the superstition that we can not be happy without paying for it.

If a man's piety makes him glum and censorious, you may be sure it is not religion. He may be moral and conscientious, a devout churchman and a fine citizen, but unless he has learned the worthwhileness of joy, he has not attained spirituality. He who says he has no time to relax, to play games, to follow the arts, to enjoy his friends, is unconsciously admitting that he has no time for living.

In the mad rush and senseless competition of modern life we tend to swallow everything and savor nothing. Before an impression is made on the heart or brain it is effaced by another.

There are few things sadder in life than the failure of human beings to know when they are happy. Man is prone to take for granted all the bountiful blessings that come to him daily, and to magnify the unhappy, discordant things. Robert Louis Stevenson, battling against grave physical infirmities, accepted whatever gaiety the moment afforded and set it afloat to cheer and inspire others. "The spirit of delight," he declared, "comes on small wings."

Helen Keller, bereft of sight and hearing, declares that she feels the eloquence of the hands she touches, often finding sunbeams in them that warm her heart.

The condition on which we enter the Kingdom of Heaven is unequivocal. Not possessions or talents or fame or power are required of us; simply that we become as little children, faithful, trusting, loving, and joyous. Irrespective of handicaps, whether mental, moral or physical, a child seeks to extract what happiness it can out of life.

With the coming of maturity the shades of the prison-house close in upon us. We can no longer depend on the spontaneous gladness born of youth and health. But there are habits which, once established, conduce to ameliorate the most unhappy lot. By keeping our eyes open to beauty, our ears attuned to melody and laughter, our minds alert to wisdom, and our hearts awake to every manifestation of love, we can not fail to enlarge our capacity for enjoyment and to widen our horizons.

The distinction between pleasures that are fleeting and joys that abide must ever be kept in mind. We can recognize the latter by the fact that they always possess an outlet as well as an inlet.

"Joy," it has been said, "is the grace we say to God." The man who has discovered the secret of living in the spirit breathes a freer, more confident air. He goes through life with a song in his heart and laughter on his lips, a source of strength and inspiration to his fellow travelers.

The Poet reveals to us hidden beauty, the Musician catches harmonies for us out of the silence, the merry hearted teach us how to smile. Gaiety carries its own passport to the human heart.

Jesus did not counsel men to be joyless, solemn, and ascetic. He hated taboos and ritual, and boldly proclaimed that His mission was to bring life and life more abundant. Throughout the Gospels we find references to the part joy should have in our lives. "Ye shall rejoice in all that ye put your hand unto." "The joy of the Lord is your strength." "Go thy way and eat thy bread with joy." And in listing the fruits of the spirit, St. Paul ranks joy as second only to love.

We are ever ready, when faced with disaster and despair, to fall on our knees and beseech help, but it is also important that we share our joys with God by offering them up to Him in humble gratitude. The test of joy is whether or not it permits of this divine participation. The Mystics perceive this truth when they declare: "In Thy Presence is fullness of joy."

Discipline

As we rise in the scale of being the anxieties and sorrows of life pass into discipline, and discipline into virtue. So, my soul, stand erect and glory in thyself and in thy God.

THE ideal man, depicted by Marcus Aurelius, is "uncontaminated by pleasure, unharmed by pain, untouched by any insult, feeling no wrong, not overpowered by passion, dyed deep with justice, accepting with all his soul everything which is assigned to him as his portion."

This pinnacle can only be reached by a process of self-control from the cradle to the grave. When you meet a man or woman who lives above the chaos of the present, maintaining a calm and constructive philosophy in the face of overwhelming odds, you may know that person has achieved this state through long and thorough discipline.

There is no meaning to the world unless it be a place where men may progress to a higher life, and there is no progress without travail. The soft, easy, parasitic life seldom produces anything but stagnation; and the gratification of our desires soon makes them our masters. The mad pursuit of money, fame, or temporary pleasure can but lead to disillusionment. Even the Epicureans knew that it was only by using discipline and self-control in one's pleasures that satiety can be avoided.

The problem of ordering our lives and modifying our temperaments is not a simple one.

We tend to shirk the effort necessary to evaluate our potentialities and develop them. The line of least resistance is a supine resignation to things as they are, including ourselves.

Fortunately it is not left entirely to us to discipline ourselves. Life does it for us. The daily round of affairs offers ample ways of chastising us, and it is not necessary to don a hair shirt and mortify the body in order to learn submission.

But while much of our discipline is compulsory, some of it is a matter of choice. Giving up the present desire for something better to come, submitting to restrictions in order to gain a larger freedom, is the part of wisdom.

It is not enough to know the way; we must travel it. Feeble, flabby muscles can be developed only by action. We should challenge our weaknesses, be they physical, mental, or moral.

The art of living is largely a matter of conscious choice. Every trashy book we read means a chance lost to read a good one; every foolish undertaking a missed opportunity of doing something worth while; every responsibility shirked a failure to acquire strength.

Iron must pass through the furnace to become steel, the field must submit to the harrow before it produces grain, and man must be subjected to discipline before he becomes of any use in the world. But a woman in the midst of a dire personal tragedy once had the courage to remark: "When the gold is in the furnace, the Goldsmith is never far away."

Any reasonable amount of suffering and sorrow is justified if a spiritual end is attained. The test of our faith in anything is our willingness to suffer for it. Worthwhile results are seldom reached except through sacrifice on the part of some one.

We do not drift to Heaven. It is necessary to take command of the helm, face the winds of adversity, in order to serve rather than impede our progress. We must visualize our goal, chart our way, then hold to the course at all hazards.

The man who refuses to submit to discipline is like a river that overflows its banks, thereby destroying the means by which it could reach the sea. Obedience to law, however, is no sign of servility. Often the finest men are those of the strongest passions—which they have learned to control.

The foundation of spiritual discipline is in getting our selves out of the way, that we may know our souls. Constant demands of the senses, petty personal ambitions, frustrations, and physical weaknesses, must yield to the larger concern with the spirit.

By directed thinking we control our actions, and the harder the habit is to form, the more permanent will it eventually become.

Once we perceive the results of our efforts, we begin to take an artist's pleasure in fashioning our lives in fairer form; and as "what we are speaks louder than what we say," we unconsciously begin to influence others. Our duty, especially to the young, is not so much to teach as to show them how to live. Children are by nature idealistic and respond readily to the appeal of beauty, love, and truth.

"But," asks the skeptic, "what is truth? How dare we affirm for them what we doubt for ourselves?"

William James, the founder of Pragmatism, answers: "The true is whatever proves itself to be good in the way of belief."

Of one thing we can be sure—self-control, relinquishing the baser for the finer, submitting to just discipline in order to attain growth, can but make for a better life.

Never before was there a time when discipline was more needed in the world. During the carnage of war, spiritual values are in danger of being overlooked. We need to train our minds to think fairly and constructively, our lips to speak temperately and truthfully, our hearts to respond compassionately to all human needs. It is only by harnessing our instincts and training our impulses that we may hope to do our part in preserving the higher ideals that are now in jeopardy.

Work

. . . Life is indeed darkness save where there is urge,
And all urge is blind save where there is knowledge,
And all knowledge is vain save when there is work,
And all work is empty save when there is love;
And when you work with love you bind yourself to yourself, and to one another, and to God.

KAHLIL GIBRAN

THE Old Testament doctrine, that work is a curse sent upon man as a punishment for sin, was happily superseded by the teachings of the Gospels that lifted it into something dignified and noble, a privilege rather than a penalty. "Labor born of desire is never drudgery," and if a task be approached with enthusiasm it is half accomplished.

If life is to be significant for us, we must be eager about some phase of it. It is only by doing some work in the physical, mental, or spiritual realm and doing it with fervor, that we acquire a zest for living.

The old adage, "All work and no play makes Jack a dull boy," can be matched by the assertion that all play and no work makes Jill a dull girl. The woman who has no aim in life, who drifts with the current, grasping at each passing pleasure, receiving more than she gives, soon ceases to have anything to give. "Life loses its savor if the salt of work is left out." Abbé

Dimnet considers indolence and gregariousness the chief deterrents to the higher life.

The other side of the picture presents the vast multitude who work too hard. Deprived of initiative and victims of the machine age, they find life little more than a monotonous treadmill.

Between the two extremes are those who dream dreams but fail to put them into effect. Worth-while things come to us only through effort on our part. Has it not been said that it is not enough to be good, we must be good for something? A lamp that does not give light or a clock that does not tell time is worse than useless. They fail of the purpose for which they were fashioned.

We can not all rise to the heights of Lord Tweedsmuir, who declares in his autobiography: "I would be content with any job, however thankless, in any quarter, however remote, if I had a chance of making a corner of the desert blossom and a solitary place glad."

By liking what we do when we can not do what we like, we are outwitting fate. A faithful perseverance linked with a gay acquiescence has changed many an irksome job into a congenial occupation. George Meredith wisely pointed out that in order to drag a log successfully one must deify it.

What a fine prayer that of Edward Thring: "Oh, God, give me work till the end of my life, and life until the end of my work!"

One of the advantages of work is the association it brings through coöperation. The disinterested effort of men, working together in a common cause, creates a unifying purpose that binds them as few things can.

The apotheosis of all work, of course, is service, and opportunities to serve come to us in proportion to our ability to use them. The world recognizes and remembers only those who have been useful to it.

The world is made up of active and passive personalities. There are the ingrowing, self-centered unfortunates who move idly along the line of least resistance, unconscious of the meaning of life and the glorious opportunities it offers.

Then there are those who use all their energies to the full, spending themselves lavishly for the good of others. No task is too great, no obstacle too high, to deter them from accomplishing their aims.

Every responsible man bears his share of the work in any organization to which he belongs, but every hour brings him other chances for service, unmerited favors that enrich both giver and recipient. There are little unremembered kindnesses that may prove the grace notes in the score of some less fortunate life.

The test of each life can be put into two questions: What do we want most? What do we want it for? If our heart's desire is the gratification of our ego to the exclusion of all else, we may be sure we have lost the Happiness Road.

It is a travesty to pray daily "Thy kingdom come" and then do nothing to help bring it to pass. Insofar as we refuse to coöperate, the work is retarded. God needs our human personalities to carry out His great design.

By, hoarding our possessions, our knowledge, our sympathies, our affections, we are not only stultifying ourselves but hindering the progress of others.

Service is not always easy. In order really to help people, we must in a measure love them, and loving brings responsibility. Human relationships are so complex, our lives so interwoven, that once we identify ourselves with others we must expect to share their sorrows as well as their joys. But by a strange paradox, it is often by easing the burden of another that we gain strength to bear our own. There are many times when we can not find help but there is never a time when we can not give it.

What we are wont to regard as hindrances—the whining beggar at the door, the tiresome complaints of an acquaintance, importuning letters from strangers—may be mere unjust demands upon our time. But, on the other hand, they may be God-sent chances for helpfulness. We should remember that a withheld blessing impoverishes us more than the applicant.

Service to others is the one field of work where there never need be unemployment. There is a job for every one, a richly paying job that brings worth-while results.

Elizabeth Barrett Browning wrote:

> A poor man served by thee shall make thee rich;
> A sick man helped by thee shall make thee strong;
> Thou shalt be served thyself by every sense
> Of service which thou renderest.

Generosity

There are those who give little of the much which they have, . . .

And there are those who have little and give it all. . . .

There are those who give with joy, and that joy is their reward:

And there are those who give with pain, and that pain is their baptism,

And there are those that give . . . as in yonder valley the myrtle breathes its fragrance into space.

KAHLIL GIBRAN

ONE of the most heartening things about the present day is the intelligent effort that is being made toward a more equal distribution of the good things of life. Endless organizations are working to improve conditions in industry and among the poor. Men and women are giving lavishly of their time and substance to raise the standard of living.

But there are still too many who are content to take from life far more than they give. They clutter their homes with unneeded possessions, seek more pleasures than they can enjoy, are generous only to those who can afford to be generous to them. To such people a gift means little more than a discharged obligation.

Even Christmas has become a travesty with many,

the prices of exchanged presents being nicely calculated to approximate each other.

Those who take the luxuries of life for granted often fail to realize what the necessities mean to others. Having should mean sharing, not only of one's possessions but of one's self. The carelessly dashed-off check, or the passing on of a superfluous garment, are helpful, but it is only when one gives also of his interest and sympathy that he meets James Russell Lowell's ideal:

> Who gives himself with his alms feeds three—
> Himself, his hungering neighbor and Me.

It is only by obeying our impulses to give to the measure of our ability that we help God answer a prayer.

A biblical passage that often puzzles people declares that "by a man's gifts he makes room for himself." Let us consider the nature of these gifts. First, take the material ones. What better sign can we show of affection than wanting to share our fortunes with others? Our hearts expand at the giving just as the recipient's heart expands at receiving, and the way is made clear for a closer relationship. A gift may be large or small, the principle is the same; adding a good book to a friend's shelf, or a plant to his garden, may express as warm an affection as a more expensive present.

But it was not of material gifts alone the writer was speaking when he said: "By a man's gifts he makes room for himself." It was of the far more precious spiritual gifts of affection and understanding, of sympathy and inspiration.

What a vast hoard of treasures each of us has to give and how little we recognize our riches! Strength to the weak, courage to the fearful, tolerance to the erring! There is no end to the blessings we can share with others.

A humble old Negro once said wistfully: "Us poor folk ain't got nothin' to give but favors." How little he realized that the true worth of a gift lies in what sacrifice it costs the giver!

Never withhold your gift because it is small. Emily Dickinson understood this when she wrote:

> They might not need me—yet they might;
> I'll let my heart be just in sight.
> A smile so small as mine might be
> Precisely their necessity.

Whatever blessing comes to us, the least we can make of it is to give it wings. It is all right to keep our griefs, if we must, but we are obligated to share our joys. Opportunities for doing this must be seized at the moment, as impulses kept waiting inevitably cool.

There is no better evidence of a generous nature than forgiveness of an injury. That is a royal gift and raises one superior to personal feelings and petty resentments. It is only the things that come through one's spirit that can reach the spirits of others.

One of the small ways in which we can constantly give of ourselves is through the medium of letters; not the perfunctory note of condolence, nor the hurried line of congratulation, but a bit of our personality which, tucked away in the privacy of an envelop, may be sent speeding on a mission of joy, or love, or sympathy.

One must know not only how to give but how to receive. Some one coined the clever phrase, "a stingy receiver," recognizing the obligation of the recipient to share the joy of a gift with the one who gives it.

Any gift, accompanied by true affection, entails no humiliation. It often takes a bigger nature to receive gracefully than to bestow.

Of spiritual gifts Jesus says: "Give and it shall be given unto you," but he adds, with a terrible inner meaning, "For with the same measure that ye mete, shall it be measured unto you again."

When He walked the earth, we are not told that He believed this or that, or observed church ordinances; but we are told explicitly that "He went about doing good."

This is within the reach of the least of us. And just as we give of ourselves, our possessions, our sympathy and understanding, do we make room for ourselves in the hearts of our fellow men.

Moods

I WANT a power to keep me from being depressed in the vale, and to prevent me from being giddy on the height.

GEORGE MATHESON

THERE are few qualities the excess of which brings so much suffering as sensibility. Were there not temperaments acutely responsive to stimuli, we would have no artists in any field. Yet uncontrolled sensibility brings unlimited misery.

Life is a compound of bitter and sweet, and to expect it to be all of either is futile. Excessive optimism is as foolish as excessive pessimism, but, used in moderation, we can gain faith and courage from the one and caution, foresight, and common sense from the other.

The fact that every thought tends to realize itself in action should make us very careful about indulging ourselves in the luxury of moods, especially if they be negative ones. Being miserable, unfortunately, can not be a purely personal affair. Like the mumps or the measles, it invariably spreads to the rest of the household.

The passion for being noticed, or the dread of being overlooked, begins in childhood and usually ends in exhibitionism. There are many who seem not only to enjoy ill-health, but to derive satisfaction out of being wretched. The dramatization of their misfortunes flatters their egos and tends to center attention upon themselves. Any failure on the part of others to appraise them at their own valuation results in a mood of depression.

We are told that our emotional reactions are frequently influenced by changes in our physical chemistry; that fluctuation of vascular pressure, increase of toxins, and acceleration or retardation of the inhibitory centers of the brain rouse us to ecstasy or plunge us into dejection.

Notwithstanding the fact that these reactions are solely earth-born, they have the power of deceiving our subconscious minds so completely that we accept them as truth and proceed to act upon them.

In mastering the mood of the moment and intelligently studying the hidden springs that actuate it, we are often able to achieve a poise that enables us to cope with real tragedies when they come.

There are many methods of combating unfavorable moods if we but have the patience to employ them. It is well to remember that we should be personal in our joys, impersonal in our sorrows. Excessive emotional reaction is dangerous hysteria, precluding any intelligent handling of a situation.

Expecting too much of life is another pitfall to be avoided. Half of our sorrows come from setting exalted standards for people and then breaking our hearts when they fail to live up to them. We do not realize that we are all in different stages of development, and that just as those below us disappoint us, so in turn do we disappoint those above us.

Indulgence in "the blues" should be regarded as a degrading, if minor, vice, and we should devise some method of consuming our own emotional smoke. Fixing our attention upon our miseries tends to perpetuate them, and by ceasing to mention them we help to banish them.

It is an accepted fact that there is no better escape from morbid self-preoccupation than in service for others.

If the stream of life is kept flowing freely, there is little chance for noisome pools of self-pity, resentment, and discouragement to form. Personal pride, hurt feelings, envies, and jealousies can find no lodgment in a healthy, vital existence.

The best of us fail so lamentably to live up to our potentialities! Regardless of race, color, creed, or personality, we each have the opportunity of performing our part, however humble, in the building of God's kingdom. Upon the links we as individuals furnish, depends the strength of the long family chain. Remember that "behind us marches an army to whom our halt means blockade!"

Emerson in his wonderful essay on *Experience* says: "Dream delivers us to dream and there is no end to illusion. Life is a train of moods like a string of beads, and as we pass through them they prove to be many colored lenses which paint the world their own hue, and each shows only what lies in its focus."

It is of paramount importance that we keep these lenses clear and bright, that they may reflect the glory of God.

Beauty

> We are sure that beauty is one with health
> When it is touched with the Eternal's wealth
> Of wonder and peace.
> Therefore is beauty the soul's true anodyne
> For all the ills that never should have been.
>
> C.Y.R.

THE longing for beauty is the soul's desire for an outward and visible sign of the unseen and the spiritual. If we can link it with God, we make of it a creative power. The artist seeks to arrest the significance of the passing moment and perpetuate it. As an Arabian poet has said:

> Beauty is eternity gazing at itself in a mirror.
> But you are eternity and you are the mirror.

The quest for beauty is as old as man. Cavemen sketched crude reproductions of nature on the walls of their habitations and sought to ornament their bodies with design and color. Later, the Greeks discovered beauty in the regular, the symmetrical, the rhythmical. Plato tried to identify it with the good; later philosophers saw it as something that pleased the eye regardless of its moral content.

Then the idea dawned that beauty was a function of life, not a mere conquest of matter by form. It was found that all beauty derives from the creative energy which renews the race. Every art, including religion, has its source in love. Children think little of beauty until they approach puberty, then objects take on a warmth and passion never before observed. This sudden apperception of beauty spills over into a desire to reproduce, not only one's own kind, but whatever appeals to the eye, the ear, the mind, or the soul. The effort thus to imprison beauty in painting, sculpture, poetry or music is, as some one has finely said, "the artist's wistful cry 'Stay longer! Thou art so lovely!' "

As our senses gradually respond to the stimulus of beauty, our eyes begin to note the symmetry, grace and color even of common objects, our ears become attuned to the song of birds, the laughter of children, the sound of the wind in the trees, the wistful fall of rain.

Far, far beyond our capacity to receive, is the bounty of beauty that the world has laid before us. Every moment yields its quota of joy to our senses. Every nerve is a channel through which beauty may reach us. Surprises await us at every turn, in the exquisite perfection of a wild flower or the majesty of a sunset.

The perception of beauty is wholly relative, varying greatly with the individual. Many can only get æsthetic thrills by proxy, needing to see the human form through the eyes of a sculptor, the beauties of Nature through the mind of a poet, the colors of a landscape by the aid of a painter. To such people an interpreter is necessary, the reproduction being more appreciated than the original.

Others gage the worth of all things by their cost. They can not perceive that for sheer beauty an iridescent bubble surpasses a costly pearl; a dewdrop under the sun eclipses the most brilliant diamond.

To sensitive, perceptive souls like Shelley and Keats and Wordsworth, the sensation of beauty was so poignant that little accidents of light and shade on the most homely and familiar things could transform them into objects of surpassing loveliness.

Schiller says: "The man who strives for inner harmony must remove himself from belittling influences, must scorn all quest for outward success, must fill himself with what the best and finest of all ages have dreamed and accomplished; he must dwell in the idea of the beautiful."

Nothing contributes more to this end than a preservation of a state of wonder; wonder at the goodness of God and its manifold revelations in the universe.

The perception of beauty is one of the most universally distributed of all human qualities. Independent of wealth, or health, or joy, it may be found in the pauper, the invalid, the most unhappy.

The fact that beauty is at one and the same time without cost and above price, robs it of the curse of possessiveness. The simple joys of earth and sky may be shared alike by all. At any moment we may look about us and enjoy the miracle of growth, the infinite variety of design and color in nature, the evanescent play of light and shadow.

Beauty thus perceived soon takes on a new and personal meaning. We learn to identify ourselves with the stars in their ordained course, with the mystery of the obedient ocean tides, with the music of wind and rain. Thus by being a part of every aspect of nature we claim our divine heritage of sharing in the ecstasy of creation.

A story is told of a little girl who, walking with her father on a starry night, was awed into silence by the beauty above her. Her father asked what she was thinking about, and she said: "If the wrong side of heaven is so beautiful what must the right side be!"

Would that we all might have that sense of wonder and awe in the presence of the Infinite!

When a man has become thoroughly beauty-conscious, it is impossible for him to regard this universe as a mere machine, driven by blind force. There is a plan and design in the world that bespeaks a spiritual universe full of intelligence and predetermined beauty. All of Nature becomes the work of a supreme artist, a superb designer, and the struggle to reproduce this beauty is but the perpetual effort of humanity to achieve immortality.

Health

Out of the vastness that is God
  I summon the strength to heal me.
It comes, with peace ineffable
  And patience, to anneal me.

. . . .

I summon the faith that puts to flight
  All impotence and ills
And that, through the wide universe,
  Well-being's breath distills.

C.Y.R.

THE word health means wholeness and derives from the same stem as holy. Health is really God's life seeking fulfilment physically through our bodies; spiritually through our souls. Never, perhaps, in history has man so needed a healthy mind in a healthy body as to-day.

When the entire network of our nervous systems is being played upon by the destructive elements of world war and our ideals are crashing about us, science alone does not suffice to maintain our equilibrium. Spirituality is necessary if we are to survive.

Christ's mission on earth was avowedly to bring life and life more abundant, and we can estimate the importance He gave to healing the sick by the time He devoted to it. Fortunately His ministry was not confined to His own day. His spirit has gone on healing down the ages.

As human beings we are limited by heredity and environment, but we possess sufficient free will to make or mar our lives by our reaction to what happens to us. The highly complicated mechanism of our bodies is subject to many maladjustments; but it is capable of direction through wise management.

On the physical side Nature provides a power that makes for health, growth, and fulfilment, tending to heal and restore the broken and injured, and often accomplishing what the most skilled physician can not. A great French surgeon, in fine humility, put over the door of his hospital:

> I dress the wound,
> God heals it.

It has taken man a long time to learn the interrelation between body and soul. A physical disturbance can express itself in mental aberrations quite as readily as ignoble thoughts and emotional disturbance can produce lesions and functional troubles. In Dr. Carrel's remarkable book *Man, the Unknown,* the necessity is stressed of unifying man's attributes and considering him as a whole.

A neurologist of wide experience made the amazing statement that he had never cured a patient who did not believe in God. A man may attain a perfect body and remain a mental or a moral invalid. It has been estimated by medical authorities in America that half the patients in the hospitals are being treated for diseases of mental or emotional origin.

Three steps necessary in healing are analysis, relaxation, suggestion. First we must make an honest appraisal of our condition. It is not enough, however, to face facts; we must see beyond them to the underlying reality and get at their cause. If we are compromising with our standards and failing to sublimate our animal instincts, we can not hope for recovery.

Second, we must learn to relax. Rebellion against sickness, losses, or poverty tends to increase their power over us. It is better to live with our handicaps than against them.

In the realm of healing, science and religion make their closest contact. The first teaches us that matter is simply a grouping of particles of energy called electrons, and these electrons are influenced by our thoughts. Religion goes on to prove that our destinies are largely in our own hands, and that "as a man thinketh so is he."

The third step in healing is suggestion. Having thoroughly studied our problem, and learned to relax in body and mind, we are ready to coöperate with God to bring about better conditions.

Accepting, as we do, the fact that our universe is governed by law, we do not believe in miracles as understood in the past. But we know that just as wonderful things are accomplished over a period of time, as were ever effected spontaneously.

Einstein says imagination is more important than knowledge, and another writer claims that "knowledge can be so literal as to distort the truth." By making an image of ourselves as we wish to be, and steadfastly holding to it, we tend inevitably toward attaining it. Says Le Comte, "We build our ideals and they in turn build us."

The same laws exist to-day that existed in the time of Jesus, and they were, neither then nor now, fully open to man's comprehension. But Jesus, being the greatest diagnostician and healer the world has ever known, foresaw the possibilities of using these laws in new and constructive ways. The fact that He did not believe His works were miraculous was shown in His assurance that "he that believeth on me, the works that I do shall he do, also."

This promise should be taken literally: first, by intelligent coöperation with the most advanced science, and then, by bringing the mind and the spirit into accord with the mind of Christ. In this way we may learn to heal not only ourselves but others.

Robert Louis Stevenson, one of the most gallant sufferers on record, said that "the truest health is to be able to get along without it."

Suffering

EVEN as the stone of the fruit must break, that the heart may stand in the sun, so must you know pain.

KAHLIL GIBRAN

ON the road of life there are many who, through infirmities of the flesh, must detour or even halt permanently.

Nature, in her protest against such adverse conditions, constantly calls attention to them, often thereby defeating her own ends. It is only when the conscious mind takes constructive hold of the body that relief may be hoped for.

There is no minimizing the devastating effect of continued ill health. To feel our horizons narrowing, our strength failing, our hopes departing, to have physical pain dominate all other sensations, often tests us to the limit of our endurance.

Pain is not, like joy, an end in itself. It is often the result of mistakes, conscious or unconscious, and carries with it self-condemnation, regret, remorse. Even when we regard ourselves as innocent of offense, our sense of justice is affronted by the fact that ignorance of the laws of health is as cruelly punished as conscious infringement.

When a pain is necessary for some desired end, we can bear it with a degree of resignation, but the futile pain that deprives us of usefulness, breaks our spirit, and renders us a burden to others, is well nigh insupportable. Few of us can rise to the heights of St. Paul and glory in our infirmities.

But even to the most sorely afflicted soul, life presents a challenge which can be met triumphantly. There have always been men and women who have risen above the most terrible handicaps and attained a height that could otherwise never have been theirs. The list of those who have practised what Herbert Spencer called "physical morality" is endless. Many of the supreme names, in the realm of art alone, prove this: a blind Milton, or Parkman, or Handel; a deaf Beethoven.

Some cults claim that right thinking is a guarantee against disease and poverty. The absurdity of this is manifest. Christianity offers no immunity from suffering, mental or physical, nor does it expect us to be free from temptation. What it does promise is that we may develop strength to bear our trials.

The terrible doctrine that God wills sickness as a punishment has been done away with, being in direct contradiction to the fact that Christ's mission on earth was largely concerned with combating disease.

While suffering comes to us through the conscious or unconscious breaking of some law, we may be sure that a loving Heavenly Father can but sympathize and suffer with us. An Arabian poet has thus beautifully expressed it: "The cup of pain, though it burn your lips, has been fashioned from the clay which the Potter has moistened with his own sacred tears."

The suffering that ennobles becomes creative. This is because we seldom realize, until incapacitated by illness, that our power does not come from ourselves. It often takes extreme physical pain to teach us the lesson of humility. At first we are outraged that the stronghold of our being should be invaded by this enemy. Rebellious and resentful, we pit our puny strength against it and resist with all our power, only to find that our action but increases our misery.

It is only when muscles relax and turbulence of mind subsides that relief comes and that we learn patience, self-control, and submission. Without the pruning knife of pain many natures would fail to yield their finest fruits.

Those who are ill, even with little hope of recovery, need not despair. Work is waiting for the frailest, work that perhaps no one else can do. Many a sick bed has proven a center from which currents of inspiration have flowed over the world. In my own city almost every philanthropic institution now in existence had its beginning in the mind and heart of a permanently bedridden invalid.

When we are removed from the fever and fret of the world and face to face with the eternal verities, life takes on a strange and sometimes beautiful significance. As our interests narrow it is in our power to make them deepen.

Jung says, "There is no coming to consciousness without pain." It is the price we pay for growing. Growth means experience, and it is only through experience that we become fitted to hold a light, however feeble, for those who stumble below us in the darkness.

Happy are we who, having fallen on the march, find a wise physician to reëducate us in the laws of health and at the same time teach us to make the body subservient to the spirit. We may never again travel with the crowd, but that will not prevent our finding our own way along the Happiness Road.

Cheerfulness

THE happiness of life is made up of minute fractions—the little soon forgotten charities of a kiss or a smile, a kind look, a heartfelt compliment, and the countless infinitesimals of pleasurable and genial feeling.

S. T. COLERIDGE

OF the more homely virtues none is more conducive to happiness than a sustained mood of cheerfulness. Those who march with a song in their hearts are not only the first to reach the goal, but they bring others along with them. It is not enough to sing when the sun shines and the road lies level. We must learn to sing most lustily when the light fades and the way grows steep.

In our failure to do this we comfort ourselves with an alibi. "I am not of a cheerful nature," we say complacently, making no effort to change our natural tendency.

So much has been said about the influence of thought upon action, that we sometimes forget the influence of action upon thought. The two are closely allied, but action is more under control than thought. If we refrain from the angry retort, the quick blow of retaliation, the scowl of hate, or the sneer of contempt, the feelings that prompt them will soon calm down. Smile, whistle, sing, play the part you want to be until you become the part you play.

The misanthrope is so occupied combating the non-essentials that he has little strength left to meet the real crises. He does not require a valid cause for his discontent, any trifle will suffice. The day is too hot or too cold, the city too noisy, the country too lonesome; food is never quite right. Such people create their own miasmic atmosphere, dwelling on past tragedies, dramatizing present misfortunes, and expressing forebodings for the future.

Fortunately, this attitude of mind is capable of correction. A transformation can not be quickly made, but the cultivation of certain mental habits will gradually effect the desired change.

The advice, "Like what you like more than you dislike what you dislike," can not be bettered. Seeing the good in things and people before you see the bad in them, leaves less time for destructive criticism.

Refraining from comparing our lot with that of those more fortunate is another step in the right direction. Our health, our possessions, our attainments, while suffering in comparison with theirs, may assume an entirely different status when placed beside the misery, disease, and poverty of the other half of the world.

The habitual attitude of our minds is either positive or negative, inspiring or depressing; as we are influenced by the moods of those about us, so they in turn are comforted or vexed, inspired or depressed by us.

Some people never see happiness except in retrospect. The good times of childhood, the friends of yesterday, the romance of youth are to them far brighter than the blessings of to-day. How foolish to live on preserved joys when fresh ones may be had for the plucking!

If we go half-way to meet good luck, it will return the compliment. The unlucky man is the one who sees himself discriminated against, the victim of some chance misfortune, set apart for unjust punishment.

Each day should be an adventure full of endless opportunities for constructive living. Once we have established a channel through which thoughts of beauty and truth may travel, the current of the world's good flows through, enriching both us and others.

Cheerfulness is a debt we owe to society, in the paying of which we receive a generous discount. We can not open our hearts to give out cheer without more cheer rushing in to take its place.

We have only to look into the faces of those about us to read what life has written there. Sometimes it is goodness, sometimes evil, in some cases the page is appallingly blank. There are all too few countenances that bespeak a happy and contented nature.

It is only in rare instances that we see a face of such shining brightness that it seems to reflect dimly the glory of God.

Personal magnetism takes different forms. Sometimes it is purely physical, a vitality that brightens the eye, animates the speech, gives grace to the limbs and gladdens the heart of the beholder. Sometimes it is mental, throwing off sparks of wit and wisdom, and exciting and stimulating others intellectually. Again it may be spiritual, pouring forth a steady radiance from within that lights the pathway of all who come near. In Jesus Christ, more than in any one else who ever lived, all these qualities were combined, making him veritably "the light of the world."

What dignity it would give to our lives if we could be used thus by God for the fulfilment of His purposes! A spirit of cheerful confidence with a tender response to human needs is an infallible sign of a Christian life.

Sorrow

The dull ox, Sorrow, treads my heart,
  Dragging the harrow, Pain,
And turning the old year's tillage
  Under the soil again.
So, well do I know the Tiller
  Will bring once more the grain:
For never a grief comes to the strong—
  Or dull despair's benumbing wrong—
But from them spring a budding throng
  Of seeds, for new life fain.

C.Y.R.

UNLESS one is afflicted with arrested development, and goes through life with the shallow, superficial reactions of a child, he must inevitably experience sorrow and tribulation, and the finer his sensibilities the more acute his reactions. Weatherhead says, "The mark of rank in Nature is capacity for mental pain."

The problem of sorrow and of evil has never been explained. Life isn't good and it isn't kind to millions of people. It isn't even just. The good, in fact, suffer more than the evil, and it is futile to look for earthly rewards.

The miracle is that man, crushed by misfortunes, exhausted by effort, blinded by sorrow, has through the ages maintained the will to live, meeting his trials with magnificent courage, displaying faith in the face of apparent failure, and struggling ever onward and upward.

In addition to the afflictions of illness, poverty, and bereavement, there are the added miseries of sin and disgrace. We suffer not only for what we have brought upon ourselves, but for what is inflicted upon us.

All too often the reaction to these evils is negative. In times of stress our minds tend to contract, our interests to narrow, our activities to abate. We even stoop at times to envy the easy, empty lives of those who have never been furrowed by trouble and have in consequence never yielded a harvest.

It is a mistake to think that it is only in the sunshine of prosperity one can find happiness. Rare and beautiful blessings blossom in "that holy ground where the shadows fall." Adversity may call out dormant powers that have never before been suspected. If we never need courage and faith, how can we develop them? Crave not the untroubled life! That way lies stagnation. To those whom God most honors He gives the largest capacity for love, and therefore the largest capacity for suffering. Who is the one who can render the greatest service to his fellow men? Isn't it he who has suffered and who therefore understands?

Were it not for tribulation there would be little need for religion. We seldom think of health until we are ill; of companionship, until we are lonely; of joy, until we are unhappy. Many souls give out sweetness only when they are bruised. Milton wrote: "Who best can suffer, best can do," and Milton spoke from bitter experience.

When, under shock of trouble, our temporal supports crumble, we turn instinctively to the surer foundations of the Eternal. But, as some one has remarked, God should never be regarded merely as an extra tire. Only through years of discipline and the habit of prayer can we command at any given moment the contact we seek.

Cardinal Mercier, than whom few suffered more, declared that "trouble accepted and vanquished gives a serenity which may prove the most exquisite fruit of your life."

The importance of preserving a positive attitude of mind through all afflictions can not be overstressed. Any experience that confers a new outlook has its value and it is within our power to obtain it. If we rebel against the inevitable, refuse to compromise with fate, regard ourselves as special objects of persecution, we shall be wrecked on the rocks of despair. But by courageously facing disaster, and accepting misfortune as a natural part of the lot of man, we can to some degree mitigate it.

One of the supreme challenges to Christian faith comes in personal bereavement.

After all the centuries man has lived in the knowledge that death must come to all, he still meets it with rebellion and bitterness and a feeling of personal injury. Yet death is often the most merciful gift of an all-wise Father. When age or illness makes life too heavy a burden to bear, when usefulness is over and only days of weary waiting are ahead, the release from life should only be regarded as a blessing.

When one is taken in the full flush of an active life it is different, but even then some inscrutable purpose may be served, which it is not ours to question.

It is useless to deny that when two people, knit together by the love of years, are torn apart by death, the wound seems too great for even God to heal. Yet if one loves unselfishly he can find comfort in the words:

> When my cup's full bitterness I drain
> This thought shall still its primal sweetness keep,
> Thou hadst the peace, and I the undying pain.

Were nothing ever given us nothing could be taken away, and unless we are willing to pay the price we are not worthy of the blessing.

"Every man can master a grief but he who has it," said Shakespeare, and the folly of telling another how to bear his sorrow is manifest.

But there are certain general truths which apply to all situations. Life must go on regardless of what we as individuals suffer, and misfortunes are no worse for happening to be ours. Millions to-day are facing death, poverty, persecution, and to each of us comes the paramount duty of adding our quota of courage and faith to a war-torn world.

Sorrow, if rightfully accepted, may bring a new significance to life, a deeper understanding, a keener sympathy, a tenderer tolerance. "The way of tears is often the way of insight."

He who has conquered the fear of life has conquered the fear of death. Without suffering there would be no need for a Comforter. The invitation of Jesus is not to the shallow, pleasure-seeking ones who drift aimlessly through life. He names his guests specifically:

"Come unto me all ye who labor and are heavy laden, and ye shall find rest unto your souls."

The Lonely Road

The road is so lonely
I can't go on.
Lie down and sleep then,
Wait for the dawn.

The road is so lonely,
Dawn will be worse.
Walk through the night then,
Nulling its curse.

C.Y.R.

ONE of the hardest stretches we are called upon to tread in life is the one we travel alone. As long as we march shoulder to shoulder with a comrade, we can often make the grade; but in the deepest experiences the soul can know, we must perforce go alone.

The tragic loss by death of loved ones, the permanent physical separation or spiritual estrangement from friends, the isolation caused by prolonged illness, come to us all and must be accepted with what faith and courage and resignation we can muster. The primordial need for companionship, for understanding, seldom finds its perfect fulfilment. Often the greatest men are the loneliest, rising like mountain peaks in solitary grandeur above their fellow men.

With this hunger for companionship it is strange that instead of treating our fellow travelers with gentle consideration, we often crowd by them with hostile glances or cold indifference.

Unpleasant as the admission is, we must face the fact that much of our loneliness is self-inflicted. With millions of human beings in the world eager to give and receive affection, why should we consider ourselves only as individuals, shut off from the rhythm of life, of importance in ourselves irrespective of our relations with others?

There is no use denying the fact that life without congenial companionship is hard to face; the ideal friendship, the perfect love are seldom achieved. But when love is not in some measure fulfilled in any human life it is the fault of that life.

When we spin about us a cocoon of egotism, we have no right to complain of being lonely. Where Self is the paramount issue, there is no room for friendship. The person who regards his own opinion, taste, and judgment superior to those of others, who demands always to be the center of attention, is wilfully building his own prison. George Meredith summed it up when he said of Sir Willoughby Patterne, "for very love of self, himself he slew."

Self-centeredness, however, takes two forms: thinking too well of one's self and thinking too ill. Psychiatrists claim that it is harder to cure the latter than the former.

Nine times out of ten a lonely person suffers from an inferiority complex, being vulnerable to every careless word, sensitive to unintentioned slights, full of small prejudices. Instead of accepting with casual indifference the give-and-take of daily contact, and accrediting people with good motives, he withdraws into himself and nurses his grievance. Self-pity inevitably follows, and once a man has arrived at the stage of enjoying his woes and liking to talk about them, he is on his way to becoming a neurotic.

Fortunately, there is a way out of the dilemma for those who have the courage to take it. The first step in overcoming loneliness is to cultivate those traits that make for self-reliance. Dependence upon any one for sympathy or amusement tends to weaken us. As far as possible we should stand erect and not permit another to bear our weight.

The next step is to learn to enjoy our own minds. "Make yourselves nests of pleasant thoughts," advised Ruskin. Books, music, gardening, the pursuit of almost any hobby can become a source of healing pleasure.

Once having become self-reliant and having learned how to manufacture our own diversions, we invariably realize that "whatever from the world we win, we want a lap to pour it in." A lap is always waiting. Whatever the value of our gift, some one can use it, and frequently the invisible, intangible offerings of affection, sympathy, understanding are the most welcome.

A distinction should always be made between being alone and being lonely. Solitude, if rightly used, becomes not only a privilege but a necessity. Only a superficial soul fears to fraternize with itself. Our unaccompanied hours may not only be times of refreshment, but opportunities to digest our past experiences, and make intelligent plans for the future. Matthew Arnold wrote:

> The tasks in hours of insight willed
> Can be through hours of gloom fulfilled.

The realization that God needs us as much as we need Him, gives us a new sense of our responsibility. He needs our lips to speak the word of comfort, our ears to hear the cry of distress, our hearts to respond to the pain of the world, our hands and feet to execute His plans.

Once we become co-workers with God in the establishment of His kingdom, we will have little time for petty personal concerns and still less time for being lonely.

Nonresistance

Resist not evil, but overcome evil with good.

FROM Socrates to Christ men have shown that passivity to wrong, forgiveness of enemies, and gentle forbearance can exert an influence not obtained by all the violence in the world.

But it is preëminently in the religions of the Orient that one finds the greatest belief in nonresistance. The Buddhist believes that when a man has achieved denial of the senses and complete renunciation his soul reaches its nirvana, its absorption into the Infinite. As one sage expresses it:

"The spirit of renunciation is the deepest reality of the human soul. When the soul says of anything 'I do not want it, I am above it,' it utters a high truth."

Mohandas Gandhi in advocating civil disobedience never advises meeting evil with evil. He harbors no bitter feelings, takes no revenge, permits no violence, submits to arrest, indignities and punishment; but he will not do what he believes to be wrong. Even though we may doubt the wisdom of his judgment—for Christ taught that we should render unto Cæsar the things that are Cæsar's—still we can but admire the courage of one who risks his life for a principle.

Jiu-jitsu, the Japanese method of self-defense, means

literally to conquer by yielding. By assuming certain postures a man skilfully uses the force exerted against him to overthrow his enemy.

In our western world with its practical altruism, its fever of activity and its fine vital urge for self-expression, the philosophy of nonresistance finds little support. Passive goodness when not accompanied by active goodness seems of little value.

The most eminent exceptions are the Quakers, those gentle rebels who refuse to kill but are ever ready to go into the thick of battle to succor the wounded, and to risk their lives in building up what others have torn down. They have taken Christ's words literally and oppose violence with gentleness, hatred with love.

On the physical plane the greatest advocates of nonresistance are to be found in the medical profession. Doctors have discovered that in treating both physical and mental disorders their best ally is a spirit of calm. As a patient begins to fight pain he endows it with power to contract his muscles, quicken his heart-beat and impede digestion. Until he learns that he can not boss Fate, and ceases to pray "My will, not Thine, be done," he has little chance for recovery.

Only by yielding our personal claims to the universal necessities of life, and concentrating not upon our handicaps but on how best to meet them, can we hope to succeed. The great drama of life provides evil, sickness, disappointments, as well as joy, and it is in our power to choose the way in which we will react to each.

Few questions in recent years have troubled Christians more than the attitude they should take in regard to war. Loyalty to one's principles and to one's country seem to conflict hopelessly. It is a terrible paradox that the word "pacifist" should have come to denote something cowardly and ignoble. Yet when aggressor nations threaten to destroy all that Christianity stands for, there is no alternative but to fight to preserve civilization.

It is well to remember that the human race is still in process of development, and incapable as yet of acting fully upon the precepts laid down by Christ. Not until men have evolved spiritually to the state in which their actions are not prompted by greed and selfishness, and until they recognize that the desired end is the greatest good for the greatest number, will a concerted effort toward that end be made and peace on earth be established. In the meantime we must content ourselves with the fact that an ignoble peace is far worse than a righteous war, and that we can regard the latter merely as a means to an end.

Jesus Christ Himself was no pacifist. He fought valiantly, not against evil but for good, overcoming hardness by tenderness, injustice by mercy, hatred by forgiveness. Darkness was of no consequence to Him; light was all that mattered.

Patience

Sorrow and silence are strong and patience is God-like.

LONGFELLOW

Patience is the best remedy for every trouble.

PLAUTUS

LIKE tolerance, patience is a passive virtue, too tame to appeal to the masses and too hard upon human pride to be popular. It has been characterized as the leanest diet upon which man can exist.

Yet the power of patience, which has been called the grace of God, lies largely in the fact that it usually wins where force fails. The man who can wait indefinitely can wear down the strength of the most belligerent opposition, for in the end a forgiving spirit disarms an opponent, and wins his reluctant admiration.

In our headlong eagerness to reach the goal we run and leap toward it, but when confronted with delays and disappointments our inclination is to turn back, defeated almost before we have started.

Yet what can a man not accomplish if he will but master the secret of steadfast perseverance? A task seen in its entirety is often so overwhelming that it is apt to paralyze effort. We falter before the time and energy its accomplishment involves. But by doing little by little, as our strength permits, not expecting immediate results, and keeping our ideal clearly in mind, we eventually achieve our purpose.

When we become impatient at the delay between our desire and its fulfilment, we should consider the fraction of time one life is in the light of eternity.

Nowhere is the lesson of patience so exemplified as by God's method in Nature; the shaping of continents, the erection of mountains, the forming of rivers, lakes, and seas. Billions of years to bring order out of chaos!

One need go no further than the nearest tree to perceive the infinite patience of the Creator. First the germination of a seed in the soil, the tiny sprout, the expanding fibers, the swelling roots, the pushing up to air and light, the first bud, the leaf, the full glory of the tree! All so slow, so confident, so infinitely persistent, and if such pains have been taken to produce the rocks, plants, and animals of the material world, what incalculable foresight and patience must have gone into the making of man?

When we are tempted to be intolerant of the limitations of ourselves and others, we should think not only how far we have come, but how far we have yet to go before we fulfil a threefold perfection of body, mind, and spirit. It is well to remember we are still evolving and that it depends upon us as individuals whether the action be accelerated or retarded.

It is not our own strength but the use of our capacities which determines the success of our efforts. The most brilliant man, lacking perseverance, will achieve less than the man of mediocre ability who applies himself with persistence to his task.

Even though supermen are born who accomplish with consummate ease things that others achieve with effort, the majority of those who have attained eminence in any sphere will testify to the fact that infinite patience and perseverance precede most worth-while accomplishment.

In the development of spiritual life especially our progress seems appallingly slow. Centuries of physical and mental mistakes have resulted in fixed habits that are almost impossible to overcome.

Only by realizing that each moment is a part of eternity, and by living it nobly and patiently, can we truly direct the course of our lives. If we regard ourselves as responsible links in the long chain of progress, the faithful performance of the duty at hand becomes a sacred obligation.

No matter how difficult, baffling, and tragic the situation in which we are placed, it will be ameliorated by facing it with what intelligence we possess, and then waiting trustingly on the will of God to effect His purpose.

Sin

Sin is the rift within the lute
That by and by will make the music mute
And ever widening, slowly silence all.

ANONYMOUS

Saints are sinners who keep on trying.

STEVENSON

THE word sin has received such a thick coat of white-wash that we can hardly discern its original crimson hue. In different ages, and places also, it has connoted different things; for most of our vices have been considered as virtues at some period of the history of the world. With us, for instance, having two wives or two husbands at the same time is reprehensible, yet there have been lands where such a state enhanced the importance of the individual husband or wife. Or consider hypocrisy and deception, which nations use to-day as glorious virtues.

Philosophers, psychologists, and moralists have defined sin in various ways. They have seen it as energy applied to foolish ends; as misdirections of the cosmic urge; as yielding to criminal instincts instead of responding to the upward surge in mankind; and some even refuse to acknowledge its existence, preferring to consider it as ignorance or the mere absence of knowledge; as darkness is the absence of light.

Nevertheless, however we define sin, there are several main ways of considering it. First, we may be intolerant of it, making no allowance for the frailties that cause it and insisting that the only cure for it is punishment. Second, we may take a too-tolerant view of it, a casual attitude which results in weakening the offender and endangering society. In contrast with both these views there is Christ's. Hating and condemning sin with all His heart, Christ was able, nevertheless, to take the most wretched sinner and by loving encouragement give him the chance to try again.

Unfortunately, sin is all too often regarded as relative. Little difference is recognized between sins of frailty and sins of deliberate intent, but great distinction is made by society between sins which it does and does not regard as "respectable." Arrogance, hypocrisy, and censoriousness are often considered as aristocratic virtues, or as mere social peccadillos, rather than as vices. Convention is used as an excuse to justify them. A cultivated, charming sophisticate, seemingly free of all vices, may be actuated by motives as base as those of a condemned criminal.

The old belief in Hell as a *place* has given way to the belief that it is rather a state of mind and that we do not have to wait until we die to suffer it. Overprolonged physical pain, degrading poverty, disgrace, and many other things may constitute for us an unhappy world of torment.

One of the most terrible sufferings we condemn ourselves to endure is remorse. Sins committed against us can be largely erased by forgiveness, which, as John

Jay Chapman says, "is love, penance and absolution all in one." But our failures to ourselves, to our fellow men and to God have power to stain the past, dishonor the present, and blacken the future.

It is one thing to be aware of our sins and quite another to know how to combat them. Chastisement of ourselves or of others is never adequate. Where penal codes are most sanguinary and punishment most drastic, crimes are most prevalent.

It is well to remember that sin does not start or stop of itself. Only an evil thought on our part can set it in action, and only a stronger good one can slow it down. God does not punish sin. He gives us divine laws for living the higher life, and it is breaking them that brings about our punishment.

We should grapple with our weaknesses before they become strong enough to grapple with us. A young sin while still but a thought can be uprooted, but when it has become deeply imbedded in desire the uprooting is a more difficult matter.

Especially is this true of sins of the flesh. Strong passions and appetites do not of themselves constitute sin; they are but elements of our temperaments for the existence of which we are not responsible. Many of the world's greatest beings have possessed excess vitality, physical as well as mental and spiritual.

But since man, and man alone, is given a conscience, he can not follow the laws of the jungle with impunity. Neither can he hope to escape temptation merely by accepting a moral code. Old instincts and young reason produce endless conflicts, and it is only when man succeeds in controlling the criminal in himself that he can hope for peace.

Our way out of temptation is first to identify ourselves passionately with the life of the spirit, then to claim the forgiveness that is promised a contrite heart. By resolutely banishing all morbid sense of guilt we can then accept the challenge of a new life.

Temptation is not the same for us all. Some through heredity and fortune are able to spend their lives in sheltered harbors, suffering little from storms within or without. Others, weak by nature, are tossed perpetually on the open sea and are there subjected to every provocation.

Each of us, however, has his own special temptations and perhaps not the least of these is the particular type of inertia, selfishness, and intolerance that comes with a sheltered life.

One of the most exalted names in history is that of David, who reached the supreme distinction of being acclaimed "a man after God's own heart." Rising from the position of humble shepherd to be ruler over Israel, he possessed superb valor and a great spiritual gift for song. Through the centuries the Psalms of David have brought comfort and inspiration to the millions of Christendom. Yet David himself was a man not only of virtues and victories, but of guilt and lamentable crime. Sin had taken as strong a hold upon him as had righteousness.

It is in the Fifty-first Psalm that David utters a model plea for forgiveness. Acknowledging his transgression first, he asks to be purged and made clean.

Then he begs that he may be allowed to forget his iniquities and have a new spirit created in him. In conclusion he promises "then will I teach transgressors their ways, and sinners shall be converted unto Thee."

Surely the gladdest tidings a sinner can find in the Bible occur in the two following assurances. "There hath no temptation taken you but such as is common to men. For God is faithful, He will not suffer you to be tempted above that ye are able; but will with the temptation also make a way to escape, that ye may be able to bear it." And then, "Come, now let us reason together," saith the Lord. "Though your sins be as scarlet, they shall be whiter than snow."

Solitude

Calm soul of all things! make it mine
To feel, amid the city's jar,
That there abides a peace of thine,
Man did not make, nor can not mar.

MATTHEW ARNOLD

It is only in our quiet moments when we are free from the static of material life that we are receptive to the divine messages that are ever winging toward us. The secret of silence was learned long ago by the most practical of all mystics, the Quakers. It was there they discerned the Inner Light that proved their guide and consolation.

Fortunately this resource is open to us all if we have the wit to use it. When the way grows too difficult and we faint under our burden, it is always possible to rest alone by the wayside, and for a moment at least, to feel God's renewing strength flow through us as it flows through plants and animals. Gradually our muscles relax, our nerves steady, and courage and strength are regained to resume our journey.

If we can make these periods of rest and meditation a daily habit and learn therein to "practice the presence of God," we will find them a controlling factor in our lives, bringing wisdom and serenity and making of our religion something dynamic and practical.

Each of us rules over an uncharted kingdom of untold possibilities, which has but one subject, who is ourself. Yet in this vast solitude we are never alone, for through it all the wisdom of the world has passed. Here poets have glimpsed dreams of immortal beauty, musicians have first heard divine harmonies, painters have conceived their loftiest compositions.

It is not necessary, however, to be a genius to enjoy this seclusion nor does one have to seek afar to find a cloister. A step aside from the thoroughfare of life, and you may discover a retreat as private as a vast forest. Even a detached mood may become a sanctuary to the initiated.

The American who probably knew most about solitude wrote from his hut on Walden Pond: "There can be no very black melancholy to him who lives in the midst of Nature and has his senses still. Nothing can compel a simple and broad man to a vulgar sadness. I never found the companion that was so companionable as solitude."

How sharply in contrast to the above is the life of those who spend their days under perpetual observation and subject to the criticism of their fellow men. Such people dart about on the surface of life like water bugs, ever seeking a new expression to efface the old one.

But even the most restless and superficial can with practice acquire a modicum of peace by spending a few hours alone each day. At first the world will continue to claim its victim, the senses will respond to every passing stimulus, nerves will twitch, and attention wander. But gradually the clamor will subside, the mind and spirit will control the body, and things will begin to be seen in true perspective. A trouble can never be seen around until it is held at a little distance.

Dear as is the companionship of friends, we must learn to dispense with it, when it threatens our periods of solitude. It is only when we are alone that we really savor life, reliving our most worth-while experiences, appreciating our blessings, and quietly planning our work for the future. A musical critic once wrote: "There is no music in a 'Rest,' but there is the making of music in it!"

We have but to watch the faces of those who have discovered these secret places of the soul, to see the inner light that illumines them. It is something detached yet keenly aware, the look of one awaiting a happy rendezvous.

The rhythm of life gives it its chief thrill. Joy is at its keenest when contrasted with sorrow; courage at its height when it follows fear; faith at its noblest when it grows out of doubt. Even the saints realized that the ecstasy of bliss usually grows out of the desolation of despair.

The very transiency of happiness enhances its worth ten-fold. Keats knew this when he spoke of

> Beauty that must die;—
> And Joy whose hand is ever at his lips
> Bidding adieu.

The physical solitude that provides opportunity for rest and meditation is but the symbol of the spiritual isolation in which one can only experience a divine companionship. Let us ever remember that:

> In the castle of our souls there is a little postern gate
> Where, when we enter, we are in the presence of God.
> In a moment, in a turning of a thought,
> We are where God is.

Tolerance

Tolerant plains, that suffer the sea
and the rains and the sun,
Ye spread and span like the catholic
man who hath mightily won
God out of knowledge and good out
of infinite pain
And sight out of blindness and
purity out of a stain.

SIDNEY LANIER

ONE of the most devastating vices that have contributed to the misery of the world is intolerance. The pages of history are black with the record of persecution, especially for any deviation from the accepted religious beliefs of the time. It is only in modern days that Christianity has permitted individual interpretation of the Bible.

Apart from the larger intolerances, there are innumerable ways in which we, as individuals, demonstrate uncharitableness toward our fellow men.

Nowhere is it more evidenced than in our attitude toward those who have taken the wrong turning in life. Without knowledge of the circumstances that led to their downfall, or the complex influences that brought about their failure, we unhesitatingly condemn their actions, and refuse to believe in their efforts to reform. Some one has defined a fault as "a weakness in character possessed by some one else." Could we but learn to criticize our own conduct with the same severity we use toward others the result would be surprising!

If you honestly believe that a man is wholly responsible for his actions, then your censure is justified; but if you accept the more enlightened viewpoint of physicians and psychiatrists, you will believe that his circulation, glands, nerves, and vital organs, to say nothing of heredity and environment, are all involved in his conduct.

In approving this course, science is but adopting the system used so long ago by Jesus Christ, who knew and practiced the ideal way. He regarded men not as they were but as they might be. By compassion and tender understanding, by recognizing their limitations both of body and of mind, He was able to love the sinner while bitterly condemning the sin. He saw human beings as bewildered, confused children stumbling down wrong paths, getting lost in bogs of wickedness. His mission was to heal them in body and soul, and get them back to a life of usefulness.

In no place is tolerance more necessary than in the intimate propinquity of the home. Differences of sex, age, ideals, and taste conspire to produce constant friction. One nagging, censorious member of a family can quench its enthusiasm, paralyze its initiative and provide fertile soil for discord. The sting of an insect may infect the blood as disastrously as the bite of a serpent, and a hard, unforgiving saint can cause as much trouble as an impetuous, loving sinner.

The recent widespread condemnation of youth was

largely the result of inventions and innovations that had taken away protective barriers from them before they had had time to develop the judgment necessary to meet new conditions. Their reaction was either one of defiance of authority and subsequent sense of guilt, or of rebellious submission—which usually ends in frustration.

The old say of the young, "They are wilful, selfish, disillusioned," not realizing that it is often the fault of their leaders. In social or college life they are often encouraged in a skeptical sophistication toward established standards of conduct in the arts or in religion. The trailing clouds of glory in which they emerge from childhood are rudely dispelled before they are prepared to face the garish light of reality.

Intolerance of youth is no more prevalent than intolerance of age. Those who are still in the full flush of health and activity are too prone to be bored with the failing physical and mental powers of their elders. They fail to realize the short span of time between youth and the day when they, too, shall be in need of tolerance, patience, and tender forbearance.

Life is a compromise at best. Conflicting forces are constantly playing upon us, rousing our emotions and irritating our sensibilities. It is only by mutual forbearance and constant vigilance that we can maintain that kindly attitude which emphasizes the good and minimizes the evil, and which refrains from calling attention to every peccadillo, but makes allowances for the foibles and failings of us all.

Life's journey for most of us, whether in youth or

age, is beset with difficulties. We stumble and fall and struggle up only to stumble again. Does it not seem incredible that under such circumstances we should hinder one another with cruel criticism, careless indifference and harmful censure?

Yet we must not forget that tolerance itself has its dangers. All too frequently it slips into lazy-minded acceptance of prevailing customs, a reluctance to pronounce any moral judgment, and a cowardly refusal to condemn a wrong that is condoned by society.

A fine distinction in moral values must be maintained, especially to-day when the very foundations of civilization are being shaken by forces that seek to abolish all freedom of speech, action, and religion. Never before has it been more important that we train our minds to be impartial and accurate, our tongues to be controlled, our judgments to be fearless, and our hearts to be compassionate. When hatred, injustice, and cruelty stalk the earth, they must be put down, but in doing so we should not lose that divine tolerance which has been called "the last triumph of the victorious soul."

Simplicity

I ask no more than to restore
To simple things the wonder they have lost.

C.Y.R.

Many of the keenest joys of life are missed through our inability to differentiate between the essential and the nonessential. For generations we have been training away from the simple elemental truths toward complicated, abstract theories. In addition to the burdens civilization has laid upon us we have, of our own accord, multiplied our physical needs, stuffed our minds with useless knowledge, and cluttered our lives with superfluities.

The average man is apt to attempt more than he can accomplish, to seek to acquire more than he needs and to exhaust himself in senseless competition. Many a poor rich woman suffers physical exhaustion from fittings, manicures, shampoos, and a ceaseless round of parties. Even youth is subjected to a bewildering program calculated to result in ennui. Excess has blunted our perceptions, dulled our appreciation, vitiated our taste. Too much rich food deprives us of appetite, music heard too often becomes banal, the wisest aphorism, through repetition, becomes a cliché.

"Money," says the cynic, "will buy anything." But

as long as money is our servant it works for us, the moment it becomes master we work for it.

Emphasis on the commercial value of things results inevitably in false standards. The simple home in which the occupants and furnishings are in harmony, and in which the home atmosphere is considered more important than convention, is often looked down upon as merely naïve and shabby.

In contrast to this is the elaborate product of the architect and decorator, where comfort is often sacrificed to style, and where conformity to the mode of the moment is considered of more importance than the requirements of the family. That evasive atmosphere which can only be obtained through objects that carry individual meaning and memory, is replaced by a correct setting for a Hollywood drama.

No home, however simple, that has been converted into a house, however grand, can hope to retain the spirit of place which is its chief charm. The dwellers in such a habitation invariably seek their pleasures abroad, preferring to pay for being bored rather than to be bored at home for nothing. Excitement for them is the food of the spiritually starved, and time is a thing to be killed. What a succession of murdered hours will the worldly minded have to answer for!

Fortunately, wealth and simplicity are not always at variance. Through those who combine the two, luxury performs a definite service without which we would enjoy few of the graces of civilization. Rare collections of paintings, great symphony concerts, beautiful buildings would not exist. Simplicity does not mean austerity and ugliness. It means an avoidance of that waste and ostentation which are the foes of good taste.

Nowhere is straightforward simplicity more valuable than in our dealings with our fellow men. As soon as we put away pride and cease pretending to be what we are not, we command the respect and confidence of others.

Philosophers, prophets, and artists have been the most successful in stripping life of its nonessentials and getting down to the fundamentals of wisdom, beauty, and truth. They have discovered the secret that when a man's possessions become his limitations, he is rich in proportion to what he can do without.

The impoverished scholar can obtain more joy from a borrowed volume than a millionaire from a well-stocked library which he never has time to enjoy. A poor musician can find delight in a piano which a rich but unmusical owner can never experience.

The man of simple tastes cultivates fewer acquaintances and more friends, reads fewer books but better ones, assumes fewer duties and performs them more faithfully. By thus doing, he attains a unified interest and singleness of purpose that does away with the superfluous. Unlike the wordly minded man, he has no need to be forever bolstered up by what others think and say and do. Conformity means little to him; he cuts through the knots of convention and dares to be himself. In doing so he brings his own seasoning to the fare of life, and maintains that freshness of spirit which is the essence of enjoyment.

Nothing has suffered more from complexity than

the Christian religion. It began not as a doctrine but as a spiritual emotion, built on an understanding of men's needs rather than on any system of logic. Christ's disciples knew nothing of the Holy Ghost, the Trinity, the Atonement; their creed was based on the two commandments: to love God and to love one's neighbor as one's self.

To-day any approach to truth except the intellectual one is considered by many as childish. Historic and scientific data or factual evidence take precedence over insight, intention, and faith.

St. Paul laid down a very definite rule by which we may judge values: "The things which are seen are temporal, but the things that are unseen are eternal." A wiser than he affirmed: "Unless ye become as little children ye can not enter the kingdom of heaven."

Friendship

In the vast web of human relations in which we are enmeshed run the golden threads we call friendships. Unhappy the man who can not follow these gleaming strands back through the years and trace the beautiful patterns they have made in his life.

People are born with different capacities for friendship. Some are content with one or two intimates, others need to embrace a multitude. Whether in a *solitude à deux* or in the companionship of many, a sorrow shared is a sorrow halved, while a joy shared is a joy doubled. The poet who wrote: "Music I heard with you was more than music" knew that strange enhancement of perception in a pleasure shared with a loved one.

When friendship looks up to a superior, it stimulates aspirations, tends to idealization or hero worship, and all too often ends in disillusionment. When it looks down, it may be tender and protective, but it is often tainted with condescension. The ideal friendship is between equals, where each shares and shares alike. That is what George Eliot happily calls "the level gage of friendship."

No matter which of these relationships exists, it can only have a satisfactory continuance if both participants observe the rules of the game. For friendship is no casual hit-or-miss affair which takes care of itself; it is a matter of adjustment, of compromise, of willingness to give and accept without thought of favors conferred.

Among the things to be avoided is the spirit of possessiveness. Holding our friends too close prevents them from growing. Nothing stultifies a person more than a demanding, jealous affection that entangles him in a net of exclusive ownership.

We have no right to invade another's privacy, nor to allow another to invade ours. In the closest relationships there should be a place reserved where none may enter without permission.

The Scylla and Charybdis of friendship are the desire to please on the one hand and the desire to help by criticism on the other. Emerson thinks it were "better to be a nettle in the side of a friend than his echo." Yet it is upon our interpretation of his motives that the world's opinion largely depends, and our very intimacy entails an obligation. When a man has given us his confidence and we know his temptations and the causes that motivate his conduct, *noblesse oblige* requires us to interpret him to others in the best light possible.

The worth of a friendship may be gaged by the qualities it engenders in the participants. Resorting to flattery and condoning weaknesses call forth all that is vain and foolish in a friend, while undue criticism and fault finding may destroy the bloom which is the chief joy of a relationship between human beings.

In the ideal friendship love, respect, and admiration

go hand in hand, each calling out the best in the other.

Taking friendships for granted is one of the surest ways of ending them. Unless nourished, they tend to wither and die. Unless we earnestly desire its continuance we should never start a friendship any more than we would a love affair.

There are, of course, connections made in childhood, before our selective faculties are developed, which possess a certain affection based solely upon continuity. But so long as we develop along different lines at different paces we can not avoid realizing "the soul's sad growth o'er stationary friends."

The basis of real friendship must ever be similarity of tastes, agreement in ideals, and congeniality of interests. But even more essential is the loyalty that can withstand separation, misunderstandings, and failures, and hold fast through all complexities.

The genius of friendship like the genius of love lies in being more concerned with the welfare of another than with one's self. But unless there results a deepening of the spirit for both concerned there can be little permanent value in the relationship.

Growing Old

I know the night is near at hand,
The mists lie low on hill and bay,
The autumn sheaves are dewless, dry;
But I have had the day.

. . .

Yes, I have had, dear Lord, the day:
When at Thy call I have the night,
Brief be the twilight as I pass
From light to dark, from dark to light.

S. WEIR MITCHELL

THE most difficult lesson we have to learn is the final one, the dread of old age being only second to the dread of death. Yet the spirit of acceptance and coöperation with the laws of nature should come with the years and bring a peace and beauty that belongs to autumn. The end of a great symphony is not filled with confusion and rebellion; instead, it is a triumphant consummation of what has preceded it.

Paradoxical as it sounds, one must begin to prepare for old age while still young. Unless we early acquire the habits of self-reliance, of appreciation for our minor blessings, and of finding constant opportunities for service, there is little chance of developing those traits when we are old. Some cynic said that "old age is but a caricature of our youth," an observation which is all too often true.

Nothing is more futile than a frantic clinging to life beyond its natural span. We may laugh at the Irishman who wished he knew where he was going to die so he could never go near the place, but it is the attitude of many of us. Increased years seldom bring more physical vigor, personal enjoyment, or opportunities for service. We have had our chance at life, and for good or ill must abide by what we have made of it. Youth does not bewail the loss of the toys of childhood, neither should maturity bemoan the withdrawal of youthful pastimes. The frantic clinging to a past decade, whether it be girlish effervescence in a woman of sixty, or boyish capers in an elderly swain, can but result in absurdity. When one has glimpsed the more permanent realities he exposes his shallowness in being absorbed in trivialities.

It is useless to minimize the discomfort of old age; failing strength, curtailment of activities, the loss of beloved contemporaries test the courage of the bravest. But there is much we can do to prepare ourselves if we but begin in time.

Much has been written about the temptations of youth, but too little has been said about the temptations of age. Captious criticism, intolerance of changing customs, susceptibility to unintentional slights, sentimental clinging to the past, complaints of physical infirmities, all contribute to the unhappiness of advancing years. Scott Fitzgerald, that incorrigible spokesman of youth, said that "the worst thing about old age was its vulnerability."

As human beings we can not expect to evade our

share of tragedy, illness, and sorrow. It is the price we pay for living, and neither hopeless stoicism nor bitter fatalism suffice to sustain us in the struggle.

Only when we feel that through all our vicissitudes some unfathomable purpose runs, and that by meeting life nobly and courageously we can coöperate in the fulfilment of that purpose, do we find peace.

Philosophy assures us there are compensations in growing old, if we have but the wit to find them. No longer must we strive to make our personalities felt, comparison with the achievement of others is no longer necessary. For better or for worse, we are what we are. Freed from many of the duties and conventions that once hampered us, we can now afford to indulge our tastes, cultivate our hobbies and live our own lives. We have more time to read, write and think; more opportunity to observe and evaluate; and, if we are lucky, more leisure to enjoy "the beautiful foolishness" of things. The human drama begins to show form and meaning, the heterogeneous events of the past to fall into pattern and evolve a plot. White is not so white, nor black so black as we thought. Subtleties and nuances are more discernible, and we are free to exercise "a heart at leisure with itself to soothe and sympathize."

Could we but cultivate a kindly tolerance toward the foibles of others, a sympathy and understanding with youth, and a serene faith in an ultimate good, we would free age of its worst terrors.

When our life's work is ended and our long journey nearing its close, we should be able to catch the light of a new dawn beyond the horizon, and to travel fearlessly, even happily, toward it.

Some one has beautifully said: "The kiss of God is upon him whose last sigh issues from smiling lips," but in order to smile at the end of the journey, one must have acquired the habit all along the way.

Love

> For life, with all it yields of joy and woe,
> And hope and fear, . . .
> Is just our chance o' the prize of learning love,
> How love might be, hath been indeed, and is.
>
> ROBERT BROWNING

LOVE, being the highest thing we know, the one perfect manifestation of God, becomes naturally the supreme quest of man. The desire for human love takes precedence over all other earthly demands; it perpetuates the race, gives permanence to human relationships, and causes more rapture and agony than all other emotions combined. Such love has its inexorable rules, the breaking of which leads to inevitable disaster, for individual happiness can never be justified at the expense of other people's misery.

It is not of this love so much as of the larger compassion that we mean to speak, the love that Forbes Robinson defines as being "the living of the best life you can conceive of for the sake of others; the purifying of yourself that others may be pure."

In a world where it is impossible not to react to men with either friendship or dislike, it is fortunate that the normal reaction is toward the former. The humblest of us reach out for some one upon whom we can bestow our affection. As members of a family, a city, a state, or a nation, we can not be isolated units, but are necessarily part of a brotherhood whose joys and sorrows we share. This privilege, while it widens our horizon and offers marvelous possibilities for growth, proves at the same time to be a baffling labyrinth, with blind alleys of hate, intolerance, and injustice, through which we can only find our way by following the guiding thread of love.

"In the pursuit of wealth," says Frederick Robertson, "or knowledge or reputation, circumstances have power to mar the wisest schemes, but where character is the prize, no chance can rob us of success."

The secret of wise living lies in wise loving. It is not necessary to wait for great occasions, for special emergencies, to express our love. It is the one commodity with which we can always afford to be extravagant. The reckless expenditure of kindliness, sympathy, and affection yields richer returns than the most careful hoarding.

The secret of a fine personality is the quick intuition which senses the need of another and rushes to meet it. Some are born with the gift of compassion, that "infinite sympathy for the infinite pathos of human life." To them the cry of distress, the unspoken plea for sympathy, the hunger of the soul never appeal in vain.

Cynics are apt to deride the efforts of idealists to alleviate human miseries with temporary palliatives. But often the binding of a wound, the easing of a single burden, the chance word of encouragement serves to start a fellow traveler again on the journey.

When compassion comes into our hearts, resentment

and blame take flight. Pity permits us to love where we can not respect; to help where we can not admire.

Love, however, is by no means always wise. Sympathy can degenerate into sentimentality, pity into weakness. Like everything else, it must submit to discipline and obey the laws of common sense.

As long as we see our fellow men as merely human, we shall be doomed to disappointment and disillusionment. It is only when we glimpse potentialities of the divine beneath the weakness of the flesh that we truly love. "The strength of an affection is proof not of the worthiness of the object, but of the largeness of the soul which loves," wrote a great English preacher.

Whatever else life does to us, we should never permit it to destroy our faith in love. The principle must be held to, even though personal experience seems to deny it.

As we ascend in the scale of living we become more and more individuated centers of the divine life, reflecting in our humble persons something of the personality of God. But the art of living, like all other arts, has its technic, and few take the pains to master it. The highest mortal love seeks neither to possess, nor will it submit to being possessed. "The strings of a lute are alone, though they quiver with the same music," says an Arabian poet.

Love can not survive neglect. Once planted, it must be carefully tended if it is to grow. No weeds of misunderstanding must be allowed to smother it, no indifference cause it to wither and fade.

The recognition of love as the supreme object of

human desire makes it a possession worthy of any sacrifice. One of the hardest injunctions Christ laid upon us was to "love our enemies." The most compassionate falter before this command. Even when it comes to caring for those outside our immediate circle we are lamentably indifferent, lapsing into that sin of impersonality that ignores the existence of those who are not of our race, creed, or station.

An ideal formula for happy living is given by Tagore:

> The perfect repose in truth,
> The perfect activity in goodness,
> The perfect union in love.

Mysticism and Communion

For the world knows not of the peace that comes
To a soul at one with God.
It is only those who are traveling on
In the faith the Master trod
Who can feel through the dark that loving hand
And, holding it fast, can understand.

ANONYMOUS

RELIGION in its highest and most intense manifestation results in the spiritual enlightenment we call mysticism. It is an emotional perception and personal experience of the immediate presence of God.

As the heights of poetry and the other arts have been reached by a Shakespeare, a Beethoven, a Michelangelo, so have the heights of communion with God been attained by geniuses of the spiritual realm.

For it happens sometimes that some one who is far advanced in the life of the spirit, transcends the physical self and attains to a vital relationship with the Divine. And having done so he is thus enabled to reach higher levels than ordinary mortals, and so to make use of the great sources of inspiration denied to most of us.

The mystical experience of such a person has nothing to do with abstract ideas concerning the nature of God, the origin of being, or the immortality of the soul.

It is a personal revelation born of a passionate desire for spiritual enlightenment and springs from a humble and childlike willingness to accept revelation.

Quakers, Quietists, Prophets, and Saints have all claimed to have attained this personal contact with God, and all declare that it has lifted them above the exigencies of the present and brought them into unmistakable awareness of the immanence of the Immanent One. If man's testimony to other things down the ages has been credited, surely the assertion of this fact should be believed.

Think of Christ, Buddha, Mohammed. It was not so much their teachings that affected their times as the imprint of their mystic personalities. Christ left no written word on which to found a religion, yet in three brief years He made such an impression on His followers that through them His influence has grown and spread for nineteen centuries until to-day it gives spiritual life even to this war-torn world.

Mysticism, in its highest meaning, is no sentimental and abnormal state. It is merely religion transcendent of all that is in opposition to the divine order. By constantly transmitting the light of God, it seeks to banish the darkness of evil.

Bergson calls mystics the forerunners of the race. "They are ordinarily regarded as unworldly," he writes, "but no more perfect men of the world exist, for the world in which they live is the whole universe."

Only a few can attain to great spiritual heights, but we can all acquire a more personal and intimate fellowship with that supreme indwelling Presence who is the source of our being. To this one of the first steps necessary is self-simplification, the purging of ourselves of all superfluous actions, sensations, and emotions. Once the physical body has faded from consciousness, the spiritual makes itself felt and the individual life is merged with the universal. "A freedom beyond friction, a calm that transcends storm," attends this mystic union.

Such achievements, however transitory, leave lasting impressions. When in the depths of sorrow or distress we feel the wind of the angel's wing, or hear the whisper of divine compassion, we gain what nothing can take away. Men who have experienced this divine assurance have transcended the direst calamities and surmounted the most tragic obstacles.

Jesus said, "I and the Father are one," and insofar as we accept and act upon the belief in God's immanence in our own lives can we make the same claim.

The mystic above all men has solved the secret of happiness, for he knows that by seeing with the eyes of the spirit, even when the physical eyes are blinded with tears, he can find peace.

Each of us should have a sanctuary, a secret place where he can set aside temporal affairs and give himself over completely to the things of the spirit. It is not necessary to seek the high altar for this. Sanctuary means only a place where God is realized, and it may be anywhere that the soul is alone and free to face itself without disturbance.

In Nature we find an ideal sanctuary. In her vast peace and sanity one's petty complaints and discontents shrink to insignificance. We do not know how she communicates her secrets to us, but alone in her presence we breathe deeper, think clearer, pray more wisely.

To be with God for an hour, a minute, or even for a second, means a renewal of life and a surer vision. After such a personal experience one knows with divine certainty where to go for strength and help in time of need.

Conclusion

Only this at last I say,
Beauty that seemed so near is far.
All men come to the end of day
And see, *beyond,* the evening star.

Where I stand was once my goal.
Now my goal is the dream I see
Over the rim of the world; and so
Goal and desire shall ever be.

Shall I lament it? Only the dead
Reach a goal that is a goal.
Eyes were meant as wings for the mind;
Distance is the breath of the soul.

C.Y.R.

HAPPINESS must never be our chief aim. Only by seeking a more spiritual goal shall we find happiness—along the way. And by spiritual I do not mean merely religious. Our supreme goal should be a state of mind in which invisible things are of more importance than the visible. In which temporal things are seen in the light of the eternal, and eternal things in the light of the temporal. In which physical desires are sublimated and in which we have salvation from our inner conflicts.

To achieve such a goal is perhaps not entirely possible. When Christ said, "Be ye perfect, even as your Father in Heaven is perfect," He knew He was suggesting an ideal beyond our attainment. But He was aware also that an ideal which we can attain is not the highest we are capable of. There must ever be hills of vision *beyond* for us to climb. "The most meager hope is nearer the truth than the most rational despair," says Charles Wagner. We must press on.

But how can we know that our goal is a good one, that we are on the right road?

Only by considering its effect upon us—and upon others.

If it is allied with all that is best in us and if that best has a vital and dynamic influence over our lives, our goal is spiritually right. If it enables us to endure pain and suffering with courage, and if it makes us quick to give and to forgive, we can be sure of it. Whatever name, religious or otherwise, we give that goal, it comes from God.

Having traveled thus far through the valleys of loneliness and sorrow; having climbed the steeps of discipline, patience, and duty; having trod the heights of beauty, joy, and love; what shall we say finally of the happy life?

Is it not one in which we have sufficient health of body to forget our bodies, and sufficient health of mind and heart to dominate all untoward physical circumstances? Is it not one in which the spiritual transcends the material yet recognizes the unfailing worth of the right use of the material? Finally, is not the happy life merely a worth-while adventure with God?

It has been said that "all the way to Heaven is Heaven," and when we remember that Jesus Christ boldly asserted, "I am the way," we realize the truth of the words.